PLANNING
AND THE HERITAGE

OTHER TITLES FROM E & FN SPON

Building Conservation Contracts and Grant Aid: a practical guide
K. Davey

Building on the Past: a guide to the archaeology and development process
G. McGill

Caring for Our Built Heritage
Conservation in practice
T. Haskell

Effective Writing: improving scientific, technical and business communication
2nd edition
C. Turk and J. Kirkman

The Idea of Building
S. Groák

Land for Industrial Development
D. Adams, L.Russell and C. Taylor-Russell

Marketing the City
The role of flagship developments in urban regeneration
H. Smyth

The Multilingual Dictionary of Real Estate
L. van Breugel, R.H. Williams and B.Wood

Property Development
4th edition
D.Cadman and R. Topping

Project Management Demystified
Today's tools and techniques
2nd edition
G. Reiss

Property Valuation
The five methods
D. Scarrett

Rebuilding the City
Property-led urban regeneration
Edited by P. Healey, D. Lusher, S. Davoudi, S. Tarsanoglu and M. O'Toole

Risk, Uncertainty and Decision-making in Property Development
P.J. Byrne

Spon's Budget Estimating Handbook
B.S.Spain

Transport, the Environment and Sustainable Development
D. Banister and K. Button

Urban Regeneration
Property investment and development
J. Berry, W. Deddis and W. McGreal

For information and other titles please contact: The Promotion Department,
E & FN Spon, 2–6 Boundary Row, London SE1 8HN, Telephone 0171-865 0066

PLANNING
AND THE HERITAGE

Policy and procedures

Second edition

MICHAEL ROSS

Former Head of Listing Branch
Department of the Environment
London, UK

E & FN SPON
An Imprint of Chapman & Hall

London · Glasgow · Weinheim · New York · Tokyo · Melbourne · Madras

Published by E & FN Spon, an imprint of Chapman & Hall, 2–6 Boundary Row, London, SE1 8HN, UK

Chapman & Hall 2–6 Boundary Row, London SE1 8HN, UK

Blackie Academic & Professional, Wester Cleddens Road, Bishopbriggs, Glasgow G64 2NZ, UK

Chapman & Hall GmbH, Pappelallee 3, 69469 Weinheim, Germany

Chapman & Hall USA, 115 Fifth Avenue, New York, NY 10003, USA

Chapman & Hall Japan, ITP-Japan, Kyowa Building, 3F, 2-2-1 Hirakawacho, Chiyoda-ku, Tokyo 102, Japan

Chapman & Hall Australia, 102 Dodds Street, South Melbourne, Victoria 3205, Australia

Chapman & Hall India, R.Seshadri, 32 Second Main Road, CIT East, Madras 600 035, India

First edition 1991

Second edition 1996

© 1991, 1996 Michael Ross

Typeset in 10/12.5 pt Trump Medieval by Mews Photosetting, Beckenham, Kent

Printed in Great Britain at St Edmundsbury Press, Bury St Edmunds, Suffolk

ISBN 0 419 21040 7

A catalogue record for this book is available from the British Library

Library of Congress Catalog Card Number: 95–74657

♾ Printed on permanent acid-free text paper, manufactured in accordance with ANSI/NISO Z39.48-1992 and ANSI/NISO Z39.48-1984 (Permanence of Paper).

CONTENTS

PREFACE

This book is intended to fill a gap. There are many books which will show you the very many buildings that go to make up our architectural heritage, but there are few that explain the legal and administrative framework that helps them to survive, or how that framework has evolved. This framework is long-established and, while its growth has been gradual and piecemeal, there is little doubt that it has been, on the whole, very effective. But even as this edition goes to press, the Government is consulting on further minor changes to the legislation.

The problem with the built heritage is knowing how to define it. The great cathedrals, castles and stately homes are obvious candidates. But the last 30 years have shown that to many people their corner shop in Victorian stock brick and the local factory denounced as ugly only 20 years ago are as meaningful as pieces of our heritage as Windsor Castle or Ely Cathedral. So, although we will deal mainly with listed buildings, conservation areas and ancient monuments in this book, we will also tip our hat to the less obvious candidates for protection and attempt, in the first chapter, to find a philosophy of conservation.

I am grateful to those who have helped directly or indirectly with this book: Roger Suddards, whose own seminal book is entitled with characteristic modesty *Listed Buildings* but in fact deals with the gamut of listed buildings, conservation areas and a great deal more besides; Tom Radice, Paula Griffiths, Ben Hall and Paul Heron, my former colleagues in the Heritage Division of the Department of the Environment, who all kindly read and provided many helpful suggestions on the text; Madeleine Metcalfe at E. & F.N. Spon, who guided this new author through the minefields of publishing; and Marie-Louise, who has had to live with my bad temper during the writing and without whom, as the saying goes, none of this would have been possible.

Michael Ross
July 1995

Chapter 1

WHY CONSERVE?

Man is a naturally conservative animal. We dislike change for change's sake and, except for the occasional break, we crave the familiar and establish routines if none exists. Fresh fields and pastures new excite us but they also make us nervous and wary unless and until they obtain their own familiarity. To cling to one's surroundings – to conserve – is simply a variation of this theme. It is as natural as the urge to protect ourselves and our families. But is it right? Can it be justified in a fast-changing world when the idea of progress, even if no longer accorded the halo of sanctity, is still considered by the vast majority of us as a given good? In this chapter, we shall examine why we wish to conserve buildings and exactly what conservation means.

There are perhaps three reasons why we wish to conserve the best of our buildings: the archaeological, the artistic and the social. The first two factors have always been with us, although their importance has grown in the last 100 years or so. The archaeological motive is the instinct to preserve something of historic interest. At its crudest, it is simply a desire to preserve the past as a curiosity. There is nothing particularly wrong with this. Probably the majority of visitors to our country houses and museums go in order to derive some entertainment value from comparing the lifestyles of our ancestors to the present day. It is the instinct that moved humans in past ages to preserve anything at all from our history where it did not have a continuing use, and it was probably the motive behind the very first conservation legislation in this country. At its best, the archaeological factor is scholarly and even, on occasion, passionate in its belief that the past can yield something for the present.

The artistic factor is similarly important. It springs from the desire to preserve something of beauty which has been built with the skill and care of the craftsman. The very first conservation movement – the Society for the Protection of Ancient Buildings – was founded, in part, as a reaction to the mass-produced excesses of

Victorian England. That we now value some of those mass-produced artefacts ourselves is simply a commentary on our own changing perceptions. In the last 30 years of the twentieth century, we have become more tolerant of architectural and aesthetic style. We no longer ignore the eighteenth century as an irrelevance as our grandparents did between the wars; we do not revile Victoriana as our parents did; and many of us have conceived a liking for inter-war styles and even – though perhaps less in architecture than with the other arts – for the post-war. There are probably fewer fixed points in our contemporary iconography than in any previous age: we are conditioned in our tastes by a rich variety of styles and we value them and seek to conserve the best examples. From medieval barns and churches through Palladian mansions and Victorian factory buildings to art deco cinemas and red telephone kiosks, popular taste in architecture has never been more varied. Our concern for the heritage – to conserve – reflects our desire to keep those styles and archetypes to which we can relate artistically.

It is a social factor, however, that has driven the cause of conservation forward so strongly in the past 20 to 30 years. Put simply, it is a feeling of unease at the pace of change and the nature of change. It is an attempt to hold on to the familiar and reassuring. In its broadest terms it can be related to the changing and diminished role of Britain in the post-war years and the growth of a positive industry in the manufacture of nostalgia in the artistic media – from L.S. Lowry through *Chariots of Fire* to the endless period dramas of contemporary television. In terms of the environment, it is related to the destruction of many of our historic centres before, during and after the war and their redevelopment in architectural styles which have won little public acclaim and which, in some well-publicized cases, have failed monstrously even as machines for living and working in.

There is of course a picture of Britain and it is familiar to all of us from calendars, books, picture postcards and our TV screens. It consists of thatched or tiled cottages in the south, paired with sleepy market towns and ornate churches, and a north comprising rugged stone cottages and the satanic mills of Blake's Jerusalem. The fact that this is a caricature, and is even accepted by most people as such, does not detract from its strength. Ask any television cameraman to produce an image to express the south, and the chances are that he will pick a Devon lane or Salisbury Cathedral; an image of the north, and he will pick a Yorkshire dale or a Lancashire mill

town. The images are reassuring and they contain, like any caricature, a certain truth.

The image comes closer to home. The Londoner may not care too
greatly if the mill is to be demolished; nor is the Yorkshireman
likely to mourn the loss of a Devon lane. But they do care if well-
loved landmarks nearer home disappear, because this endangers
their identity.

The image changes again. We all of us care if a feature, not necessarily even a landmark, disappears after years of familiarity.
Whether the feature is of any interest or not is irrelevant. We knew
it. We lived with it. It was part of our being. Without it, we feel a
little less whole, a little less comfortable. Suddenly, we wish we
could have prevented its going. We are conservationists.

Conservation movements are very much produced in reaction to
change. The first conservationists were resisting the excesses of the
Industrial Revolution: a second wave came in the 1920s and 1930s
as new development took off again and the unplanned growth of
towns threatened the countryside and swallowed up whole villages
and towns on the edges of our greater conurbations. Finally, in our
own time, the handiwork of the Luftwaffe followed by the comprehensive rebuilding of so many of our towns and cities and
continuing urban expansion have produced the third and greatest
wave of conservation reaction.

The law has reacted to the conservationist pressure, but it has
been able to protect only the best of our buildings (and more
recently our most lovely areas). To the man or woman in the street
lamenting the demolition of their local cinema or the house they
were born in, the legislation must seem criminally inadequate. For
them, the protection of the best architecture seems academic. If
change means for them their displacement from well-known and
well-loved surroundings to an out-of-town housing estate or a tower
block, their feelings of alienation may become a social or even a
medical problem. The difficulties experienced by people who have
been affected this way lie outside the scope of this book, but they
are familiar to anyone who has dealt with conservation questions
and in particular the psychology of conservation.

The politicians have ignored conservation at their peril. They
started after the last war with the noblest of motives to rehouse a
population many of whom had lost their homes to the bombers or
who lived in sub-standard accommodation. The post-war age was
the great era of central planning. Mother always knew best, but in

this instance mother was the Government or the local authority. Much of what they did was excellent. Much of what they did was necessary and humane. But its effects were sometimes successful only in solving one ill by creating another.

Perhaps it was not the face of redevelopment but the way it was carried out that now turns the blood cold. Communities uprooted, decanted and reassembled produced an understandable hostility and this in turn has been responsible for much of the vandalism and more serious anti-social behaviour with which we are all too familiar. The new communities that were planned were often soulless – unending grids of streets and courtyards, often entirely lacking in social or even shopping facilities. Then there were the tower blocks, which were good for some but a living hell for others. Corbusier's drawings, as fine and fantastical as the Italian futurists of the early years of the century, often became built nightmares in the hands of lesser architects acting for councils with an overriding interest in cost. The aftermath of the Ronan Point disaster in 1968 simply accelerated their rejection by most of society.

Those new communities that succeeded – and some did succeed – did so because they were successful in recreating a sense of community which, even where it had not existed, was associated with the old houses and towns that had been left behind. Oddly enough some of the much criticized tower blocks are now themselves becoming success stories under the impact of new central and local government initiatives designed to improve their fabric, provide the amenities that should have been provided in the first place (such as entryphones and adequate lighting in public areas), and to create a new sense of community. By the late 1960s, there was a loss of confidence in modern architecture and it has never since been regained. The architectural profession has been notoriously bad at defending its own corner. When tested, architects have not always proved able to answer their critics. For a time in the mid-seventies, when the conservation movement was gaining ground, it seemed as if the well-designed new building was one that tried its best to disappear from view altogether by hiding behind landscaped features or curtain walls of blackened glass. Community architecture – which was little more than the architect heeding what the users of his building told him about what they wanted – was treated as revolutionary and in some quarters as a form of deviancy. The architects' response to public revulsion against modernism was the toytown delights of postmodernism, with its silly ornamentation and false decoration.

It is small wonder that against this background the emphasis should turn from new build to restoration and refurbishment and it was actually found in many cases to be cheaper. Since the late 1960s, comprehensive redevelopment and clearance have dropped slowly out of the housing vocabulary. Repair and improvement have become the buzz-words. To conserve is better than to redevelop. The successful man or woman aims to buy an old cottage or house in the country where in the mid-thirties they might have commissioned a Maxwell Fry or a Walter Gropius to build them a concrete cube in the Home Counties. The magazine racks have blossomed with Traditional this and Period that. The architects' own magazines are not even generally available, unlike their counterparts on the Continent.

There is another point, and it is an important one. A Picasso is hung in a gallery. Beethoven belongs in the concert-hall and can be silenced by turning the knob of a radio. But architecture is all around us. It is the only genuinely popular art form. We cannot shut our eyes to it. We must not only live with it but in it, and unless we have the wherewithal we usually have little choice in the matter. It should be the most democratic and popular of the art forms, and the fact that modern architecture has so few admirers and the traditional styles so many is a vote not only on what is best liked but also on what actually works.

Traditional architecture is not only familiar to us but to coin a phrase it mixes well. Britain has few towns which are set pieces of one style of architecture. Most streetscapes consist of a variety of architectural styles from different ages; there are, however, certain conventions. They are likely to retain the same building line; they are probably built or faced with similar materials or, if these are different, there is usually a pleasing sense of variety. There will almost certainly be a little ornamentation, even if it is only on cornices or around windows and porches. Compare this to the street where a piece of insensitive modern architecture has been introduced. The building material may be unsympathetic; the building will bulk large, and ornamentation is likely to be lacking. Any new building is likely to obtrude by its very newness.But it should be capable of complementing its older neighbours. There should be a dialogue between them. The bold architectural statement has its place, but the average High Street is the wrong one. Good, sensitive modern architecture – once scathingly referred to as Heritage Year infill – certainly has a place, and those who practice it have found plenty of clients over the last few years.

Has the pendulum swung too far? Are we in danger of turning the country into a huge conservation area? There are certainly strong economic arguments against keeping heritage buildings up at any cost. Industrialists who find themselves located in a listed building may simply find it uneconomic to maintain. At worst, their livelihood may be threatened and removal to new premises may be impracticable or too expensive. Again, we might question whether the constant imposition of aesthetic judgements about what is of special architectural interest is wholly compatible with property-owners' rights to do what they like with their own property. Finally, will there ever be an end to the Government's programme of producing lists of historic buildings enjoying statutory protection, or to local authorities' designation of conservation areas where lesser degrees of control apply?

The Department of the Environment has done its best to answer these fears. Listing and inclusion in a conservation area place few new burdens on owners, and the listed building consent process exists to test among other things the economic viability of maintaining a listed building. But the doubts remain. Only a tiny percentage of our total building stock may be listed, but the figures seem to continue to expand. A nation that regained some of its self-confidence in the 1980s and is committed to economic growth on the free enterprise model may find the idea of onerous state and local authority controls anathema. The Conservative Government since 1979 has done much to streamline planning controls, especially in those growth areas which may be suitable for designation as Simplified Planning or Enterprise Zones. Has the time perhaps come when the conservation of the built heritage should similarly be given a new look and a halt called to the increasing numbers of buildings and areas enjoying protection?

We shall attempt to answer these questions in the ensuing chapters. Conservation has had a good press over the last 25 years for the reasons we have been advancing. But the development that is prevented at the last moment by a late spot-listing; the householders who find their double-glazing contract is worthless until they receive consent for the work to their newly-listed house; the owners aggrieved that their house has been listed without their being able to comment on the proposal and fearful of its implications – these are the sort of individual problems that need to be addressed, not least because the individuals concerned are unlikely to be unscrupulous property developers. In fact, Government has addressed these questions and has managed to produce satisfactory solutions in most cases. But the days when the conservation movement had a clear run of public opinion are long since gone. There are respectable arguments against conservation and they must be answered intelligently. Where they cannot be answered, they should be attended to.

Perhaps the key to the pro- and anti-conservation arguments is the word conservation itself. In the dictionary, it has a very similar meaning to preservation but, so far as historic buildings and architecture are concerned, there is a difference and it is more than a semantic one. Conservation has come to allow for the possibility of change – for the better – where preservation has retained its original sense of pickling. The difference is most evident in the legal definition of conservation areas, which are defined as areas of special architectural or historic interest, the character or appearance of which it is desirable to *preserve or enhance.* Similarly, the act of listing does not mean that a building must necessarily be preserved in its original state for all time (although there is a presumption against change). The listed building consent process allows for works of alteration or extension, especially where these enhance the chances of preserving the building. As we shall see, there has been almost a growth industry in finding new uses for old buildings. Departmental circulars extol the practice, architectural books demonstrate the practical aspects, and architects themselves have been responsible for some remarkable work, all in the name of conservation and its implication of change where change is due.

This change of emphasis is itself due at least in part to the growing pressure that we have experienced in the heritage field over the past 35 years or so. Early legislation thought merely in terms of preservation – as in Building Preservation Orders, which preceded the present listed building controls. But two sorts of pressure have acted to change matters. In the first place, the speed and intensity of development have forced on us the necessity of either adapting our old buildings to new uses and modern standards or of sweeping them away. Not unnaturally, we have chosen the path of adaptation, and that route now has the blessing of official policy, as we shall see. Adaptation in this case means not only the most dramatic cases of old buildings being found totally new uses requiring a certain amount of internal and even external alteration. It also means bringing old buildings into line with the needs of the late twentieth century – in terms of safety standards and in simple terms of central heating and other forms of comfort. Achieving this in a way that allows the building to keep its special interest is one of the challenges that the local planning authority conservation officer as well as the individual owner and his professional advisers must face.

The second pressure has been the sheer growth in the numbers of listed buildings and conservation areas. Our appreciation of the heritage has accelerated partly as a reaction to the pressures of development, but it has itself produced a challenge to society. Developers have found increasingly that the sites they wish to develop are occupied by listed buildings or are situated in conservation areas, and that their plans may accordingly be opposed not just by local protesters but by the planning committee. There has been a pressure on them to adapt their proposals, to make use of the buildings that they find on-site or to design new ones that are in keeping with the character and appearance of the surrounding area. Sometimes to their surprise, they have found that this is cheaper than total redevelopment and produces more pleasing results. The challenge has been to the architect and the planner to find the right result in each individual case. Most often, the end-product has been a good old-fashioned British compromise – but it has been none the worse for that. The days when the architectural profession castigated infill architecture have gone: but so too have the days of the diehard preservationist for whom to remove stone from stone of any listed structure was a confession of vandalism. It has been a long and hard-fought contest, and in some quarters it still goes on. But conservation now allows for the possibility of adaptation, and it has gained a respectability with everyone involved with the development system, and is no longer the concern of a single lobby.

That is perhaps the greatest tribute to the way that we care for our heritage in this country. The numbers of listed buildings and conservation areas have both grown fourfold since the early 1970s. Both are often to be found in urban centres where development pressure is greatest. There are still battles between the developer and the conservationist: the Mansion House Square proposals in the City of London and the controversy over the foundations of the Rose Theatre in Southwark were witnesses to that. Significantly, both were in central areas of the capital where property prices are high. There are plenty of local contests too as most amenity societies would testify. But the idea of conservation, the presumption that the old must survive – and on occasion adapt – has triumphed. The notion of the continuing community, one which acknowledges the value of much of its past and treasures its qualities, has taken root in architecture and planning as it has in other areas of life. We prefer organic change to radical change and on occasion we prefer no change at all. Much damage has been wrought to our historic centres in the process of coming to this conclusion: whole communities and areas have been cleared away, and not always because rehabilitation and restoration were too expensive an option. The philosophy of conservation, however, *is* accepted by the majority; architects, developers, planners and politicians cannot ignore this fact.

Chapter 2

THE RISE OF THE HERITAGE

2.1
The beginnings

When did conservation begin? If the music-hall song is to be believed, not by the time of the Civil War and all those ruins that Cromwell knocked about a bit. Curiously enough 1660 acts as something of a watershed for us, for it was after the Civil War that the first glimmerings of a new sensitivity about historic architecture can first be detected with the flowering of English medieval research and Anglo-Saxon studies.

John Aubrey's *Chronologia Architectonica* of the 1670s was one of the first works of architectural history in the English language and attempted to establish some sort of progress in the development of English medieval architecture. Anthony Woods' *Antiquities of Oxford* (1674) was in much the same vein, as was the snappily-titled *A Survey of the Cathedrals of York, Durham, Carlisle, Chester, Man, Lichfield, Hereford, Worcester, Gloucester and Bristol* (1727) by Browne Willis. For the first time, it seems that writers were turning their attention from places and events to architecture, and in particular to that fascination with Gothic architecture which was to inspire so many in the eighteenth and nineteenth centuries. There was not as yet any desire to conserve old buildings (the purists will recall that at this very time Sir Christopher Wren was adding a contemporary extension to Hampton Court quite out of keeping with the original fabric); but at least someone was taking an interest. Following this came the foundation of the Society of Antiquaries in 1717 and the charmingly-named Society of Dilettanti in 1733, taking up and forward the theme of the gentleman scholar.

The trend towards scholarship, while never universally taking hold, began to affect architecture and the way that society – or at least one wealthy portion of it – viewed the past. In the late eighteenth and early nineteenth centuries, the torrid tides of the romantic movement held sway over the fashion-setters of the day, clashing but usually with happy results with the classical aspirations of others. For the country-house builders, well-sited ruins and groups of cottages became essential elements in the landscape. This was the age of the picturesque: there was nothing particularly conservationist about it. If the ruins were not in the right place, they were built as new. If a group of buildings spoiled the view, however charmingly dilapidated, they were moved. But at least it was a start. Here was the first recognition that the past was not something entirely to be passed over or destroyed. Perhaps it was their exposure to vistas of Roman ruins on their Grand Tours that caused so many of the great men of the day to begin to be interested in their own past.Starting with Gothic architecture (and chiefly ecclesiastical rather than secular forms) historic buildings began to be a source of pride rather than scorn.

Economic forces, however, were predominant, and the Industrial Revolution paid scant regard to the preservation of old buildings or much else for that matter.The newly-rich factory owner (who often enough was already a member of society's 'upper crust') usually performed as his first act the acquisition of a family seat and its improvement or embellishment in the style of the day; and a very good job he often made of it too. Both these 'improved' older houses and the new homes constructed by these industrial magnates feature extensively among the lists of historic buildings that we have, but such acts hardly marked a concern to preserve the best of the past.

More controversial was the later, Victorian mania for 'restoring' churches to what was felt to be their Gothic origins. In all too many cases, this meant degutting the building and recreating the interior in high Victorian style rather than the medieval Gothic it sought to emulate. Puritan England may have whitewashed the walls, but no-one destroyed the fine interiors with such gusto as the Victorians; of course we now preserve their vandalism as an architectural form of its own.

It is difficult from all this to see much serious interest in practical conservation before about 1870. By that time two things had happened. First, the worst excesses of industrialization had provoked a reaction among an intelligent élite who saw that the changes of preceding 150 years had wreaked a havoc of their own on the physical face of Britain. These people were not dyed in the wool reactionaries, although some of their numbers did show a partiality for a Merrie England that in reality had not been so very merry for anyone. Secondly, Britain had undeniably become a great power; and like an old industrialist reflecting from an armchair on his success began to take an intelligent interest in its own beginnings.

This was no concerted national movement, but in the last 30 years of the nineteenth century it is possible to see the beginnings of a conservation movement. The first sign was the foundation in 1877 of the Society for the Protection of Ancient Buildings (SPAB). Its moving spirit was William Morris, polymath and socialist, whose art forms are admired by a new generation today. The stimulus for the Society's foundation, appropriately enough, was Morris's horror at the proposed 'restoration' of Tewkesbury Abbey. The Society's object was explicit. It intended not just to preserve ancient buildings but to ensure that their fabric was restored in keeping with the original, using where possible traditional methods and materials. The Society acted in accordance with its views, and carried out modest but worthwhile work: Inglesham church in Wiltshire is one example and bears a plaque recording Morris's work. It is a tribute to the quality of Morris's vision that not only does the Society remain true to its principles today, but for the first 50 years of its existence it was almost the only national body dedicated to the preservation of historic buildings.

2.2
The first legislation

Voluntary effort, however, was not enough. It was time for the law to step in, and true to form it did so rather late and to no great effect. But the Ancient Monument Protection Act 1882 became the first piece of conservationist legislation to reach the statute book. It gave the protection of law to 29 monuments in England and Wales and 21 in Scotland; because these were set out in a schedule to the Act, they have been known as scheduled ancient monuments ever since. Even this modest measure encountered hostility during its passage through Parliament, but at least it was a beginning.

2.3
Recording the heritage

Protecting ancient buildings was one thing, but it was necessary first to identify them and to take non-statutory action to preserve them – in other words to campaign for their preservation in the way that is all too well-known to the twentieth century conservationist. The task of identifying those buildings worthy of protection was first undertaken in London. The moving force here was the slightly eccentric figure of Charles Robert Ashbee, a leading figure in the Arts and Crafts movement of the time and a disciple of Morris. True to his beliefs, Ashbee founded a Guild of Handicraft at Mile End in London. Here, in 1894, he set up the Committee for the Survey of the Memorials of Greater London, with himself as Chairman. The purpose of the Committee was 'to watch and register what still remains of beautiful or historic work in Greater London and to bring such influence to bear from time to time as shall save it from destruction or lead to its utilisation for public purposes'. The Committee's immediate aim was to compile a register of all the most interesting buildings and to produce a series of monographs on the most important of them. The first such monograph appeared in 1896 and was given the suitably didactic title of *The Trinity Hospital in Mile End, an Object Lesson in National History*. The hospital in question was a group of almshouses proposed for demolition by the Corporation of Trinity House and then thought to be designed by Sir Christopher Wren. So from the outset, the conservationist movement was embattled.

The survey was taken over by the London County Council, which in 1898 obtained from Parliament the power to buy historic buildings or to provide funds for their restoration and maintenance. It is an interesting reflection that central Government was not to give itself this power until 1953, and a further nine years were then to elapse before all local authorities were given grant-making powers. The survey has proceeded with a painstaking and sometimes agonizing slowness first under the aegis of the LCC and latterly under the control of the Greater London Council. Upon the abolition of the latter, it passed, together with the rest of the GLC's historic buildings staff, to English Heritage.

The Survey of London began as a voluntary effort, and in 1895 perhaps the most successful voluntary society of all in the conservation field was established: the National Trust for Places of Historic Interest or Natural Beauty was founded by Octavia Hill. In 1907, the Trust was given the right to hold land inalienably – no-one can acquire it without the leave of Parliament. It was also given the task of promoting 'the permanent preservation, for the benefit of the nation, of land and buildings of beauty or historic interest'. In fact, for the first 40 years of its history, the Trust was to concern itself more with land than with buildings; but that did not prevent it from doing much good work and from laying the foundations of its present success.

The next major landmark was the inception in 1904 of the Victoria County Histories (VCH). These ranged more widely than architectural history and embraced subjects as diverse as geology and natural history. Like the Survey of London, at least in their earliest days, they were scarcely based on a scientific approach, but they were another sign of a more systematic and methodical way of looking at the nation's heritage: they remain an invaluable source of local historical facts for contemporary researchers. The VCHs do in fact overshadow other similar all-embracing vade-mecums that appeared during this period, such as the Little Guides that flourished between 1900 and 1924.

Perhaps the biggest landmark of the time came in 1908 with the foundation of the Royal Commission on the Historical Monuments of England (RCHM). This was founded

to make an inventory of the Ancient and Historical Monuments and constructions connected with or illustrative of the contemporary culture, civilisation and conditions of life of the people of England, excluding Monmouthshire, from the earliest times to the year 1700 and to specify those which seem most worthy of preservation.

The prejudice against anything that was built after 1700 was all too typical of the time. Georgian architecture was considered very ugly and not worth mentioning let alone preserving. A similar prejudice can be found in many of the guide books of the day. Victorian architecture, particularly that of churches, was mentioned frequently; but that which came immediately before was almost invariably ignored completely. It was not until 1921 that the RCHM made the radical advance of substituting 1714 for 1700; not until 1946, after many of our finest Georgian buildings had been lost in the inter-war period, that the date was moved forward to 1850; and it was not until 1963 that the date was removed altogether. This chronology itself is an interesting reflection of changing public taste.

With all this activity on the conservation front, the law was long overdue for overhauling and extension. The original 1882 Act had been followed by a further Act in 1900, but its fairly elementary provisions were still intact. The Ancient Monuments Consolidation & Amendment Act 1913 was a milestone in conservation legislation and introduced concepts that have been on the statute book ever since. Section 1 allowed the Commissioners of Works or a local authority to purchase an ancient monument – a provision which had been available to the London County Council since 1898, as we have seen. Section 3 introduced the concept of guardianship to ancient monuments. This was the idea that the care of a monument, but not its ownership, might be vested in a public authority. Such a notion must have seemed radical to a society in which the rights of property owners were sacrosanct. In practice, guardianship has worked very well as a practicable approach to the problem of monuments that were of no interest to their owners, who were in any case ill-equipped to give them the careful maintenance that they required. Guardianship is with us still and has been one of the success stories of British conservation (see Chapter 7). Finally, the 1913 Act established the Ancient Monuments Board as the expert committee to deal with the care of monuments, with a membership drawn from the learned bodies and societies. Parallel bodies were set up in Scotland and Wales, and these remained substantially intact until the sweeping reforms carried out in 1984.

2.4
Between the wars

The emphasis was still on monuments and the social and economic pressures that emerged in Britain after the First World War put new strains on the whole built heritage. There were simply not enough pressure groups and voluntary bodies in existence to stem the tide. Those that did exist did what they could, and scored some famous victories; but except in the most outrageous and well-publicized cases, there was not as yet a groundswell of public support to sustain their work. In the case of buildings constructed after 1700, public opinion does not seem to have been out of sympathy with the dating criteria adopted by the Royal Commission.

One of the most serious threats came almost immediately after the end of the War. In 1919, the Church of England proposed the demolition of no less than 19 churches in the City of London. Of these 13 were built by Wren, and others were by architects such as Hawksmoor. The proposal was based on a report produced by a Commission appointed by the Bishop of London, Dr Winnington Ingram. The report argued that the churches should be pulled down because they were no longer paying their way: the sites, then as now extremely valuable, would then be redeveloped. It took seven years to defeat the proposal. The Church of England was a mighty opponent, and the resources of the conscrvationists were small. The National Trust, the London Survey Committee and the SPAB gained important help from *The Times* and from some prominent individuals like the architect Sir Reginald Blomfield. Even then, and despite mounting public opposition, the Church's proposals were passed by the House of Lords by 71 votes to 54: it was only due to the good sense of the Commons that the measure came to grief by 124 votes to 27.

The conservationists, however, did not always win. In the ycar the City churches were saved (1926), the London County Council proposed the demolition of John Rennie's lovely neo-classical; Waterloo Bridge across the Thames. Once again, the conservation lobby mustered for action and were once again led by Blomfield. This time, they persuaded the Commons not to vote the money necessary for the demolition work; but it was not enough. The LCC went ahead and destroyed the bridge anyway and replaced it with another that was to be itself demolished by German bombs in the London blitz.

The Commissioners for Crown Lands also played their part in the destruction. They pulled down Nash's Regent Street and planned to replace Carlton House Terrace with a Portland stone facade. It was this last proposal which at last brought into being the Georgian Group (originally the Georgian Group of the SPAB) in 1937 to lead the fight. The Group's founders were Robert Byron, an intellectual who had made his name as an enthusiast for the rather more exotic splendours of Byzantine architecture, and Lord Rosse. In one of those lovely ironies in which the history of conservation abounds, the architect of the Carlton House Terrace scheme was the very same Sir Reginald Blomfield who had led the earlier fights in defence of Wren's churches and Waterloo Bridge. Fortunately for all of us, this was a battle which Sir Reginald and the Crown Commissioners lost and Nash's terrace remained intact; and Sir Reginald's best-known design today is that of the electricity pylon.

The formation of the Georgian Group was witness to the slow rise of eighteenth and early nineteenth century architecture in the estimation of at least the experts. Suitably enough, the first monograph devoted to Nash was published in 1935 (it was by the 31 year old John Summerson, who was to write so lucidly about Georgian London in the years to come). Perhaps it was the rash of debased classical Beaux Arts buildings designed for business and commerce (and above all for show) that sprang up in London in the inter-war years; perhaps it was the loss of Regent Street; perhaps it was just the passage of time: but whatever the reason, it was clear that the developers were henceforth not to have things entirely their own way.

The *Architectural Review*, though in broad terms a partisan of the Modern Movement in architecture, was one of the warmest opponents of the destruction of Georgian London. In 1937 it published a polemical piece by Byron (later also published as a pamphlet) entitled *How We Celebrate the Coronation*. In this, Byron catalogued the range of buildings, mostly if not entirely classical in style, which had either recently been demolished or which were under threat. He listed in fine style those who he thought were the offenders:

The Church; the Civil Service; the Judicial Committee of the Privy Council; the hereditary landlords; the political parties; the London County Council; the local councils; the great business firms; the motorists; the heads of the national Museums – all are indicted.

Byron was by no means alone. Another contributor to the *Architectural Review* was the young John Betjeman who, at this time at least, mixed a love of Georgian and early Victorian styles with a regard for the best of the new and revolutionary architecture that was reaching Britain from the continent and America. In 1933, Betjeman founded the Shell guides and ensured that they paid due attention to the architecture of the eighteenth and early nineteenth centuries as they described England county by county.

The redevelopment persisted: in Chelsea and St John's Wood, and in many other London areas too, luxury blocks of flats were replacing streets of pretty if unremarkable housing from the previous two centuries. Outside of London, the position was just as bad. This was the England of ribbon development, of new arterial roads, bungalows and suburban sprawl. Today, we are more tolerant and even fond of Metroland and its Tudorbethan architecture. It is hard to remember that in the 20s and 30s there was an almost unparalleled takeover of greenfield sites. The county of Middlesex disappeared under bricks and concrete, and London took bite-sized chunks out of Surrey, Kent, Essex and Hertfordshire as well. Provincial cities replicated the trend to a lesser degree, and much was swallowed up and demolished that might today have been listed or included in a conservation area. Osbert Lancaster, whose work forms a cartoon chronicle of the middle years of this century, caught the spirit well in *Progress at Pelvis Bay* (1936), as did the architect Clough Williams-Ellis, in more serious vein, in *England and the Octopus* (1928).

However, we have left to last perhaps the most poignant loss to our heritage during this period. This was the demolition of so many of our country houses. If we mean by this term not just the stately homes but also the more modest manor houses of England, the sort you would once have expected to find in almost any English village or hamlet, then we can look to have lost something like 400 houses between 1920 and 1955. This was the figure cited by the organizers of the 'Destruction of the Country House' exhibition held in 1974: and if we accept that few of Hitler's bombs fell in rural areas (so that it is unlikely there was a peak between 1939 and 1945) then we can speak of an average of 13 country house demolitions a year on average for each year between the end of the First World War and the mid-1950s. If we think of the public outcry that now greets any proposal to demolish a listed building, perhaps we can appreciate not simply the scale of the loss but the lack of popular reaction to each demolition as well.

The country house had been endangered before. The agricultural depression that had taken place between 1873 and 1896 resulted in some demolitions as a result of the (relative) impoverishment of their owners, but at that time many others seem simply to have been let and their owners moved to more modest accommodation. The position of the country landowner after the First World War (and even more after the Second) was quite different. Demolition seemed to many to be the only option and there was no-one to gainsay such a decision, let alone provide an alternative solution. The National Trust were warned of the destruction of the English country house by Lord Lothian, speaking at their Annual Meeting in 1934, but by the outbreak of the Second World War the Trust still had only two country houses in their ownership. It was the Trust's Country House scheme that was to save many of our finest mansions (and some of the more modest too) from demolition. During the interwar period, however, the Trust seems to have lacked the means to finance any sort of rescue operation.

The reaction of Government was muted and predictably very cautious. Both the Housing, Town Planning, Etc. Act 1909 and the Housing, Etc. Act 1923 allowed town planning schemes to take account of 'objects of historical interest or natural beauty' and 'the special architectural, historical and artistic interest attached to a locality', respectively. However, no action appears to have resulted from either measure. There was a further Ancient Monuments Act in 1931, and more importantly in the long run (although its short-term effects were not great) the Town & Country Planning Act 1932. Among other things, this measure for the first time extended protection to buildings other than ancient monuments. It gave local authorities the power to make preservation orders for buildings of special architectural or historic interest, which meant that protection could now be extended to occupied structures as well as those unoccupied ones that had long enjoyed protection under the ancient monument legislation.

But the protection of the 1932 Act was far from good. In the first place, it relied totally on local planning authorities. In the second, each preservation order required the approval of the Minister, who had in turn to consider the representations of all those involved. Finally, there was provision for the compensation of everyone affected by the order. Parliament was reluctant to interfere with the rights of property owners, and it was an adventurous, not to say brave, local authority that made much use of the act. Certainly, it proved inadequate to the task of defending the heritage in the 1930s from the threats that were posed to it.

2.5
The Second World War

Ironically enough, the next big push in the conservation field was provided by the biggest single threat the buildings of Britain had ever faced – the Blitz. The lists of historic buildings we have today are supposed to have had their origin in the information prepared for salvage teams operating in the aftermath of the German raids. Pressed by constraints of time and manpower, they had to assess their priorities and one way in which this could be done was by preparing lists of the area's historic buildings, so that they could enjoy a newly-won importance. In fact, if this occurred anywhere, it is unlikely to have had much effect on national policy; if some inspired local authority or ARP officials did possess such lists, their link to the statutory ones prepared long after the cessation of hostilities seems tenuous. But it is a good story and it would be nice to think there is some truth in it.

A much more real and valuable side-effect of the Blitz was the foundation in February 1941 of the National Buildings Record. Spurred on by the devastation of so many historic buildings in the air raids, the aim was no less than a complete photographic survey of historic buildings. It was set up in All Souls College, Oxford, with Walter Godfrey and John Summerson as its directors. It lives on as the National Monuments Record under the aegis of the RCHM and it has still not – unsurprisingly – completed its task of obtaining a photographic record of the nation's historic buildings, but that, it must be said, is due in part to the fact that our definition of a historic building has widened since 1941, not least to include some buildings that were not even constructed then!

One further effect of the National Buildings Record was the publication in 1942 of *The Bombed Buildings of Britain* by Summerson and J.M. Richards, another graduate of the *Architectural Review*. It was only one of a rising tide of books looking with nostalgia at the English scene. The trend had begun before the War, when Batsford started their *The British Heritage* series and *The Face of Britain* books, now the mainstay of the British topography section of many a second-hand book dealer. But the War increased the nostalgia quotient considerably. Rupert Brooke may have wondered during the previous conflict if there was honey still for tea, but few others seemed to have wondered about the English way of life in quite the same way as those caught up in the Second World War. But then, no-one was attempting to destroy Britain's morale with air raids in 1914–18 (aside from the Zeppelins). The *Britain in Pictures* series was one of the first to echo or exploit, depending on your point of view, the nostalgic trend. Betjeman, in that series in 1943, sighed nostalgically for what he had left behind:

Not the most magnificent scenery, misty mountains, raging seas, desert sunsets, or groves of orange can compensate for the loss of the Corn Exchange, the doctor's house, tennis in suburban gardens, the bank and the bank-manager's house, the rural garages, the arid municipal park, the church clock and the Jubilee drinking fountain. Even a town like Wolverhampton looks splendid through Memory's telescope ...

English Cities and Small Towns

The reality of course was much more likely to have been nearer the vision conjured up by the shrewder eye of George Orwell in *Coming Up for Air* – a small country town sprouting badly or unplanned suburbs, with its surviving historic buildings modernized and restored unsympathetically; but no matter. Absence makes the heart grow fonder, and the Britain that servicemen abroad remembered was strong on heritage, even if the half-timbered houses they recalled were more likely to have been in semi-detached Motspur Park or Mottingham than in Ludlow or York.

The other side of the coin was the construction of the new Britain, where health, wealth and work for all meant among other things yet more arterial roads cutting through the urban landscape and yet more sub-Corbusian visions of how we should all live. What before the War had been the idealistic dreamings of the extremist MARS (Modern Architectural Research) group of architects was now entering the currency and speech of the mainstream and even the Government. The Greater London Plan parcelled London up into neat little packages and the future of old buildings within them was uncertain. Maxwell Fry, writing the planning section of the popular magazine *Picture Post*'s 'Plan for Britain', saw the old town church set in a neat field and surrounded by highways and blocks of modern flats. It all looked like a progression from Orwell's dystopic vision of 1938.

What came to the rescue – although it proved to be more of a salvage attempt in the tide of redevelopment that was to sweep Britain in the late 50s and 60s – was the post-war penchant for central planning. The years after the First World War had been ones of disillusionment: many wondered what those who had fought had suffered and died for and there was a determination that it should not happen again. The return of Attlee's Government guaranteed that in economics, in health care, in social security and in land use, central planning was to have a crucial role. The reality, as we know, did not always match the theory. Centralism, however, won the 1945 Election, and central Government was accountable through Parliament to an electorate who did not wish to be betrayed as many had felt betrayed after 1918.

Central planning also stemmed naturally enough from the war effort; and it had been seen to work and to work well. It was in fact the Town & Country Planning Act 1944 that introduced the concept of lists of historic buildings. The Act gave power to the new Minister of Town & Country Planning to prepare lists of buildings of special architectural or historic interest for the guidance of local planning authorities. Now, and for the first time, occupied historic buildings were put on the same footing as ancient monuments. Given our longstanding reluctance as a nation to interfere in the property rights of the individual, and given that many of these occupied buildings werc to be houses – and given that an Englishman's home is his castle – would such a step have been taken in another age, when the idea of planning and (a frequently necessary step in wartime) the transgression of individual rights in the wider national interest was less acceptable? It is difficult to say; but the slowness of the public response to the destruction of historic buildings in the 1930s makes one pessimistic: it could have been well into the 1950s or even 60s (when we got around to the idea of protecting areas of special architectural or historic interest) before our historic buildings received protection, and by then who knows what damage might have been done to the heritage?

2.6
The 1947 Act: the first survey of historic buildings

The rigours of wartime Britain meant that nothing initially was done to undertake a systematic survey of the surviving heritage and by the time this became possible a further planning act was upon us. This was the great Town & Country Planning Act of 1947, which laid the foundations of the regime that we have today. The 1947 Act altered the Minister's power to compile lists into a statutory duty. Owners were given no right of appeal and were simply told that their property had been listed. Nor was there any compensation payable. These aspects have lasted to the present day. The Act was weaker on the control of work to listed buildings – although it still represented a significant advance on what had gone before. The law provided that a listed building could not be demolished, nor could major works be carried out to it, without two months' notice being given to the local planning authority. During that period, the authority could serve a Building Preservation Order. This had to be confirmed by the Minister, but once confirmed, it usually provided for the authority's consent being necessary before any work specified in the Order could be carried out. The Order also empowered the authority to require the building to be restored to its former state (an interesting provision in itself) and was supported by penalties for any breach of its provisions. Ecclesiastical buildings and ancient monuments, then as now, were singled out for special treatment.

Just as important as the passage of the Act, 1947 saw the first national survey of historic buildings get under way. There was really no precedent for this. It was the first time that anyone had undertaken such an ambitious exercise. To be sure, the RCHM's painstaking inventories, carried out county by county, were designed on much the same lines. It was the very slowness of the RCHM's work, however, that had made a separate national survey necessary. It had to be conducted with a little more speed, not just for the sake of efficiency and economy but also because sooner or later (in the event it was later) all those visions of a new Britain would come to pass, and the identification of the heritage was a priority.

In fact, the first national survey took 22 years to complete. There were many reasons for this, not the least of which was that the very job of examining the thousands of towns and villages and investigating the richness of the architectural heritage was a task which those planning the exercise must have found impossible to gauge. In the first place, who was to undertake the exercise? There were few enough architectural historians around, still less enough of them able and willing to undertake lengthy spells of fieldwork in the byways of English vernacular style. The salaries were scarcely excessive and the travel and subsistence a constant source of niggling and haggling between Whitehall and those in the field. As a result of these factors, the survey was conducted by a mixed team, whose eccentricity and occasional lapses were more than compensated for by their scholarly work and their initiative. They were given the delightful title of investigators, and their head was the Chief Investigator. The shades of the amateur sleuth were not wholly lacking. Little enough was known about much of the architecture that they had to inspect. Architectural history was still at a fairly elementary stage. Enough was known about the best work of the best architects, but there was a lack of reference material for much British architecture.

It is a parody, but it is difficult to get the picture of the lady or gentleman amateur in their Morris 1000 entirely out of mind when thinking of the investigators. Many performed the work on a voluntary or near-voluntary basis. Many of the entries for villages comprise simply the church, the 'big house' (if it survived) and any other building of immediate interest or note. Smaller buildings were hardly touched at all. Anything built after 1800 was lucky to get a look in. One imagines a summer's afternoon; an inspection of the village church; tea with the squire in his garden; and a return home in time for dinner at seven. No doubt quite unjust, but nonetheless irresistible.

In fact there were serious gaps in the survey lists, as subsequent work during the second nationwide exercise has shown. But it is important to remember that the investigators started from a low knowledge base, and for that matter with public taste unknowing and uncaring about much vernacular architecture. This was after all an age in which our own generally pro-conservationist prejudices were unknown. If the work of the investigators sometimes seems superficial it was at least in part because they were not required to supply anything else.

A more serious charge against the first survey was its almost total neglect of Victorian architecture. The pendulum had swung far from those days at the turn of the century when High Victorian was still very much to be revered – usually at the expense of the eighteenth century. Gothic architecture was out and it was very late in the survey that it received its first look in. The investigators were simply reflecting the prejudices of the day. Perhaps indeed it was the very losses of Victorian buildings in the redevelopment schemes of the 1950s that brought them back into fashion. Betjeman again was one of the leading lights who helped bring the resurrection about. He was one of the sponsors (along with Lady Rosse, wife of the co-founder of the Georgian Group 20 years before) who helped to establish the Victorian Society in 1957. The immediate cause of the Society's foundation was the destruction of the ornate entrance to Euston station that year. There were to be many other battles in the years to come but the Society were not ploughing barren ground. Their membership grew from under 600 in 1961 to 1700 by 1968 and to nearly 3000 by 1978, and the lists of historic buildings began to reflect this revived interest in Victorian architecture.

By the end of the first survey in 1969, almost 120 000 buildings had been given statutory protection. Nearly 5000 were in the top Grade I and the rest were in the subsidiary Grades II* and II. A further 137 000 buildings had the non-statutory Grade III to their names; this was no guarantee of protection, but at least it marked them as having some local interest whenever a local planning authority came to consider proposals affecting them. The lists were confusingly divided into 'provisional lists' which contained brief – usually very brief – descriptions, and 'statutory lists' which gave the name and address of the owner. Printed on white foolscap that rapidly became dog-eared with use, the lists were hard to read and difficult to follow, but at least they were a start and in many areas they were all that stood between the local heritage and the bulldozer for the next 20 years.

2.7

Conservation in the 'age of the bulldozer'

The national survey of historical buildings was not the only conservationist step that the post-war Government took. In 1946, the Chancellor of the Exchequer, Dr Hugh Dalton, established the National Land Fund with £50 million obtained from the sale of war-surplus items. The purpose of the Fund was to preserve historic buildings and natural landscape as a celebration of the newly-won peace. The fund never quite matched the high aspirations of its creators, and in 1957 it was arbitrarily reduced to just £10 million.

More importantly, the first steps were taken to end the sad destruction of so many country houses. The Gowers Committee was appointed in 1950 to consider

what general arrangements might be made for the preservation, maintenance and use of houses of outstanding historic or architectural interest which might not otherwise be preserved, including, where desirable, the preservation of a house and its contents as a unity.

The resulting report recognized that Government had to step in and provide incentives and relief for those owning historic houses. Government grasped the nettle and the Historic Buildings & Ancient Monuments Act was passed in 1953.

The Act did two main things. First it made specific provision for Government grants for the repair and upkeep of historic buildings – the first time that buildings, as opposed to monuments, had been treated this way. In 1953 itself, grants totalled £250 000. Secondly, the Act established the Historic Buildings Councils for England,

Wales and Scotland. These paralleled the long-established Ancient Monuments Boards, and advised the Minister not only on grants but on listing policy as well. The Government thus gained access for itself to the leading scholars of the day – a source of architectural advice that permitted them to keep in touch with public taste and private scholarship.

These developments were a hope for the cause of conservation. They still took place, however, against a backdrop of massive re-development that swept away much that was good and substituted some of the most mediocre architecture that this country had ever seen. Whatever else can be said of the 50s, they were not a decade of distinguished buildings or distinguished builders; and yet the end of the building licences systems in 1954 (essentially a form of rationing of materials) could have been, perhaps even should have been, the beginning of an age of good architecture. Why there was no Wren, no Haussman, to preside over the rebuilding of London or the bombed provincial centres of Britain has been the source of much speculation, most of it inconclusive. Macmillan's call for an annual target of 300 000 new homes at the start of the decade at least answered a well-documented social need resulting from war damage and a recognition that many of the population were living in sub-standard accommodation; but the redevelopment of so many of our cities in the 50s and early 60s brought more questionable gains. Is Bristol's Broadmead shopping centre an environmental asset? And was the rebuilding of Newcastle in the 60s an architec-tural success? The isolation of John Wesley's chapel in the former and the damage done to Eldon Square in the latter suggested that it was not. Even where (as with Wesley's Chapel) the building itself might be preserved, its setting was not. The reason perhaps is that we are speaking of a different and more confident age when progress was still considered to be progress, and the icons of the present had more attraction than the curiosities of the past. What planning authorities did in the 25 years after the end of the War they did, by and large,with the acquiescence of the vast majority of their citi-zens. It is only a more puzzled and less confident age like our own which shudders at the neat concrete cubes that massed and piled formed the centres of our bomb-damaged cities. To be fair, there were success stories: Plymouth, Coventry, Norwich (where old and new have been blended with special success) – these are the more popular manifestations of modern architecture and town planning. Some of the new towns shared the success, from Stevenage to

Milton Keynes. The idea that all planning has been bad planning is fallacious. The best has been a successful merging of old and new.

Good planning acquired a new ally in the 1950s. The Civic Trust, established by Duncan Sandys MP, won early fame by fighting developer Jack Cotton's scheme for Piccadilly Circus. By the mid-1960s it had 700 local affiliates – civic and amenity societies that tapped a deep sense of local pride and used it in the interests of good design. The Trust was to emerge as both a valuable pressure group in the interests of conservation and a force in promoting good modern design. It had and continues to have its work cut out.

There was one further source of encouragement, this time in the cause of conservation education. This was the publication of Nikolaus Pevsner's *Buildings of England* series. These were a worthy successor to the county guides of the turn of the century, filled with wonderful scholarship and a liberal dose of heavy prejudice. The émigré Pevsner persuaded the publisher Allen Lane to produce the guides, and they appeared in 46 volumes between 1951 and 1974. In convenient pocket form, they made the nation's architectural heritage accessible to all. Pevsner's lucid prose and down-to-earth style did much to educate a public that was beginning to awake to the concept of heritage. Sometimes under threat, the series always managed to keep going and survive as a worthy memorial to their author.

As the 1960s progressed, it was clear (at least with the benefit of hindsight) that existing legislation was not enough. In particular, although it was possible to protect individual structures through the ancient monuments and listed buildings systems, it was not possible to protect the character of whole areas. Public concern focused on individual outstanding cases, like the demolition of Euston Arch in 1961 and the Coal Exchange in London in 1962. Pevsner called the first 'villainy' and the second 'stupidity' (both were demolished in the course of improved transport schemes). It is doubtful if the legislation was at fault in such cases. More worrying was the fate of the historic centres of Britain where whole areas of architectural value were under threat. As the 1960s went on, it was to these that the Government turned its attention.

Chapter 3

HERITAGE COMES OF AGE

3.1
Conservation areas

It is one of the oddities of conservation in this country that it took 20 years to move from the protection of individual buildings to the protection of whole areas of special interest. It was true that, as we shall see, buildings could be listed for their group value, but the idea of going beyond this to consider how whole areas could be preserved seems to have taken root late in the day. This is curious, given that the Housing Acts of 1909 and 1923 had allowed – without effect – for town schemes to include provision for areas of special character; and curious too in that the planning system in this country has always considered proposals for development – any development – not just on the grounds of their intrinsic merit but also in relation to their effect on the general amenities of the environment locally and, on occasion, nationally.

The first faltering step in the right direction came in 1966 when the Government commissioned the Four Towns Reports. These were four separate studies, each carried out by consultants, which were designed to establish ways in which the erosion and destruction of historic towns might be stopped. The studies were supposed to provide solutions for specific local problems and lessons capable of more general application to historic centres. Bath, Chester, Chichester and York were the four towns chosen, and although the solutions prescribed were difficult to extend to other centres, the studies were useful in pinpointing the particular problems that faced such communities: economic pressures; the need to find new uses for old buildings; traffic; and the special problems of finding finance to deal with the problem of decay. Here were four case studies sponsored by Government which were produced by well-respected experts: surely now Ministers would act?

They did act, but with a curious degree of caution. They set up another committee – the Preservation Policy Group (PPG) – which took until 1970 to report. The Group was set up to coordinate and consider the Four Towns Reports; to review experience elsewhere and abroad; and to recommend legal, financial and administrative arrangements for preservation. In their Report, the PPG said

We do not think it would be an exaggeration to say there has been a revolution over the past five years in the way old buildings are regarded, and in the importance now attached by public opinion to preservation and conservation.

The Group's main recommendations were that local authorities should be able to initiate conservation schemes in the knowledge that central Government grants would be forthcoming. It was to be another two years before Government acted on that.

But the Government had been active on other fronts. The establishment of the Four Towns studies was the first indication that Government was taking a lead on conservation. The Ministry of Housing and Local Government report *Preservation and Change*, published in 1967, was another. It painted a frightening picture, pointing out that at the then rate of redevelopment, every town in the country would be rebuilt over again in 50 years, and that the rate of change was accelerating. The twentieth century, said the report, had brought countless benefits to town dwellers, but it had wrought much damage too. Many buildings of grace and distinction had been demolished, and pictured alongside this statement were the Coal Exchange and Euston Arch, destroyed with the acquiescence of Government only five and six years before, respectively. The report pointed out that no-one was against change, but that the preservation of areas of architectural or historic interest should be compatible with change. Nor did this mean simply saving just listed or other older buildings. It meant looking at the whole physical composition of historic areas – the size and proportion of the buildings, their alignment and roof-lines, their detailing, texture and colour. Local authorities were encouraged to carry out townscape surveys and to develop conservation policies for these most sensitive areas. The lavishly illustrated and cogently written *Preservation and Change* is one of the better publications to emerge from Whitehall and was the first of a series of positive and helpful pieces that gave (and indeed give) good advice on conservation matters.

Most importantly, local planning authorities had a new tool in their armoury. This was the conservation area, and *Preservation and Change* warmly commended its use. The genesis of the conservation area is generally supposed to have been the case of *Iveagh (Earl of)* v. *Minister of Housing & Local Government*, which reached the Court of Appeal in 1964. The case involved two adjoining terraced houses in St James's Square in London, owned by the Earl. Building preservation notices had been served on the grounds that their alteration or demolition would have a detrimental effect on the square. The Earl of Iveagh challenged this: the point of contention was whether a building should be listed for its intrinsic special architectural or historic interest or whether it might possess such interest simply by virtue of its setting as one of a group. The Court of Appeal came out in the Minister's favour, but it was a divided decision, and one that left the conservation world, and no doubt the Government, rather rattled. The result was a Private Member's Bill which became the Civic Amenities Act 1967. It was introduced by Duncan Sandys, MP and had the vigorous support of the Civic Trust. Local authorities were now given a statutory duty to

determine which parts of their area ... are areas of special architectural or historic interest the character or appearance of which it is desirable to preserve or enhance and shall designate such areas.

So the conservation area was born, and became an important tool in the battle against unrestrained development. There are now over 8000 conservation areas, and the controls applied to them have guaranteed an extra layer of protection for buildings within them. Perhaps most importantly, local authorities had for the first time a weapon that they could use to help preserve the character and appearance of their best areas: the Minister had only to be notified of the areas that were designated: he/she did not even have to be consulted.

3.2
Legal developments 1968–74

The next year, the Town & Country Planning Act 1968 strengthened the legal protection given to listed buildings. The existing rather cumbersome machinery was telescoped, and the list itself effectively became a building preservation order, so that any building on the list became automatically subject to listed building control. The term 'listed building consent' entered the planners' vocabulary for the first time. For buildings which were not already listed, the Act provided a new power for local planning authorities whereby they could serve building preservation notices that would have the effect of temporarily extending listed building control to the building until the Minister had had a chance to decide whether to list it permanently. These provisions are substantially those that survive today. Owners now had a great deal more certainty about the controls that existed over their properties. They knew – and know – that once listed they were subject to the consent procedure straight away. The Damoclean sword of the building preservation order was taken away.

There were two further significant changes associated with the 1968 Act. First, Crown buildings became eligible for listing for the first time. This had always been something of an anomaly, since they had long been scheduled as ancient monuments whenever this was appropriate. Crown buildings were still not subject to listed building control (although a substitute consultation procedure was soon promulgated and became accepted); but at least now they were marked as being of special architectural or historic interest, and given the large numbers of historic buildings in the ownership of the Crown this was an important advance. The second change was the recognition in the Ministry of Housing & Local Government Circular 61/68 of conservation area advisory committees. These committees, to which we shall return in Chapter 7, are local authority bodies but having only consultative status. Their foundation was in line with the idea behind conservation areas that their designation, protection and above all enhancement can only be achieved with a high level of public participation and help. The committees, by bringing together local residents, councillors, business people and representatives of the relevant professional associations, ensured that local authorities were at least aware of public and professional views. The establishment of the committees remained a matter of local authority discretion, but many were set up and they have become one of the minor success stories of the history of conservation in this country.

The 1968 Act, important as it was, was not to stand for long. Its successor Town & Country Planning Act 1971 was to become the major and long-standing statute for all planning legislation, albeit with substantial amendments and additions over the years. In the conservation field, the listed building controls survived intact and were supported by powers permitting local authorities to serve repairs notices on the owners of listed buildings, and to back these up where necessary by compulsory purchase, and by further powers to carry out urgent repairs to listed buildings themselves and to recover the costs from the owner.

A year later came the first piece of amending legislation – itself perhaps a sign of the speed with which conservation interests were being reflected in Government. The Town & Country Planning (Amendment) Act 1972 followed up the recommendations of the PPG that central funds should be available for mainstream historic buildings conservation schemes as well as for the repair of outstanding buildings. Section 10 of the new Act permitted the Secretary of State to make funds available by way of grant or loan for work connected with the promotion, preservation or enhancement of outstanding conservation areas. The definition of 'outstanding' was to be fixed by the Historic Buildings Councils (HBCs), and in concept was similar to the grading of listed buildings. In 1965, the Council for British Archaeology had prepared a list of 324 historic towns, 51 of which were 'so splendid and so precious that the ultimate responsibility for them should be a national concern'. In practice, the HBCs assessed the status of conservation areas as and when they received grant applications falling within them, or following an approach from a local planning authority. For those that received the accolade of outstanding status, there was the prospect of up to 50% Exchequer grant, again in line with the PPG's 1970 recommendations.

The second reform introduced by the 1972 Act was the control of demolition of unlisted buildings in conservation areas. It is perhaps typical of the gradualist approach of the British, particularly in the case of controls affecting property rights, that the form of control was by means of a direction – a system rather akin to the old building preservation order which had just been abandoned in the case of listed buildings. In any case, this rather cautious approach was soon pushed aside. The Town & Country Amenities Act 1974 substituted automatic control over the demolition of any building in a conservation area, with the exception of those to which listed building control did not extend (such as churches in use) and those for which the Secretary of State issued a direction about their exemption. In

The sort of buildings overlooked in the first survey: *top*: dog kennels;
bottom: a fine medieval barn interior.

its way, the Act was almost as sweeping as the reforms of the Town & Country Planning Act in 1971. Here, in one swoop, control was extended over the 2000 or so conservation areas then in existence, and perhaps just as significantly the Act, which had been a Private Member's Bill introduced by Michael Shersby, MP, had gone through Parliament with Government support. The Act was highly ambitious. It introduced powers for the Secretary of State to designate conservation areas himself (which in practice he has never done) and for him to direct local authorities to produce schemes of enhancement for their conservation areas (again, never used and later repealed). It also introduced useful provisions extending the existing powers over the lopping or felling of trees to conservation areas as well as provision for the special control of advertisements, again with special reference to conservation areas. All in all, the 1974 Act, for so slim a piece of legislation, was quite a landmark in the extension of conservation controls.

3.3
Environment and conservation

The welter of legislation that was passed between 1967 and 1974 reflected a change in the public mood. Conservation, which had previously been regarded largely as an interesting byway of planning, was now centre-stage in the public consciousness. The development and redevelopments of the 50s and the 60s had not ushered in a brave new world. The new roads and urban motorways had failed to keep the traffic moving, and even where they had the public mourned the loss of the communities that had been swept aside to make way for them. Whatever the truth of the matter, contemporary architecture was perceived as a massive failure and the new demons were the architects and the planners. Of course it was an over-simplification; of course, there was good new architecture and successful new planning, but it was a little difficult to see if you were 19 storeys up in a tower block or if your home was about to make way for someone's idea of a road improvement. The white heat of technology had given way to cool reasoning about its effects. progress was no longer a platitude. The conservation movement was coming of age.

Some of this flavour accompanied the incoming Conservative Government in 1970. The architect of that white hot technology,

Harold Wilson, had been defeated, and the new administration showed itself responsive to the public mood. It established a new Department of the Environment which brought together the Ministry of Housing and Local Government, the Ministry of Public Building and Works and the Ministry of Transport – the three Government departments that most impinged on one another's areas of environmental responsibility. The MHLG, with its responsibility for planning, including conservation, was concerned in particular about transport planning at a time when road-building was proceeding apace. By putting all three Ministries under one Secretary of State, it was hoped that the conflicts between the often competing interests of good planning and good transportation could be resolved; and that putting the civil servants in one Department would lead to exchanges of ideas and a better understanding of each other's positions. We will return to this theme in the next chapter.

At local government level the new legislation brought about the birth of the conservation officer. It was clearly becoming increasingly important for local authorities to have access to specialist advice on conservation matters, especially when it came to the practicalities of devising suitable schemes for the restoration, conversion or extension of historic buildings. The Department of the Environment itself enjoined local authorities to obtain access to specialist advice – either by the employment of a conservation officer or by using the good offices of county preservation staff (where they existed) – in Circular 46/73; and they followed this up by writing to authorities to find out exactly what arrangements were being made (the Circular had asked authorities to inform the Department of their arrangements, but the response had been patchy). In some historic towns, like Chester and Bath, the conservation officer rightly had an important place in the planning hierarchy: in other centres, the position was less happy, and the break-up of some of the old county-level teams on local government reorganization in 1973–74 had worsened matters in a few areas. The Government's gentle pressure secured an improvement before Anthony Crosland as Secretary of State for the Environment declared that the party was over for local government and that restraint would henceforth be the order of the day.

Certainly, the impetus in favour of conservation did not cease with the passage of the Town & Country Amenities Act in 1974. In the same year, the Victoria and Albert Museum in London staged a successful exhibition on 'The Destruction of the English Country

House'. In vivid form, it chronicled the loss of Britain's rich heritage of country-house architecture this century, together with the loss of gardens and contents. It was estimated that over 250 houses had been lost since 1945 alone, although the demolitions on a large scale, as we saw in the last chapter, began in the 1920s. The exhibition focused on a particular and very dramatic aspect of the need for conservation-minded policies; and it demonstrated that if the issue was to be tackled seriously, then a range of measures, including fiscal and other financial ones, would be necessary. Conservation was too big and important to be left simply to the planners.

3.4
European Architectural Heritage Year

Much the same lesson came out of European Architectural Heritage year (EAHY) which was declared in 1975. The designation was the work of the Council of Europe, and it is perhaps a sign of the changing times that European Conservation Year, which they had declared in 1970, had contained not a mention of the conservation of the built environment. The high-sounding aims of EAHY were:

To awaken the interest of the European peoples in their common architectural heritage;
To protect and enhance buildings and areas of architectural or historic interest;
To conserve the character of old towns and villages;
To assure for ancient buildings a living role in contemporary society.

The Chairman of the International Organizing Committee was Duncan Sandys, and the UK Committee had the Duke of Edinburgh as President, the Secretaries of State for the Environment, Scotland and Wales among the Vice-Presidents and the Countess of Dartmouth as Chairman of the Executive Committee. The British campaign had three aims:

1. to carry out work in all of Britain's conservation areas, then numbering about 2000;
2. to inaugurate a campaign of environmental education;
3. to launch a revolving fund for the restoration of historic buildings.

On all three counts, EAHY met with success. The first objective was met with the award of Heritage Year Grants which were first announced in Circular 46/73. These were drawn from a fund of £150 000 (£140 000 for England, £10 000 for Wales) and were to be used in non-outstanding conservation areas. There was £20 000 for Scotland, but nothing for Northern Ireland. The England and Wales allocation was later increased to £180 000 and heavily over-subscribed. In addition, EAHY saw the initiation of a number of voluntary projects which probably achieved rather more in total than all the grants awarded. On the education side, much promotional work was achieved, not least Lady Dartmouth's own *How do You Want to Live?*, an evocative and profusely illustrated book which was published by HMSO. The Civic Trust announced a non-competitive Heritage Year Award, and 275 of them were subsequently given to selected projects.

Oddly enough, in spite of the anti-élitist approach of EAHY, the pilot projects that were selected for the UK were all rather untypical. One was the work done in Chester, an outstanding historic centre which had a long record of good work in the conservation field; one was a large-scale scheme in the centre of Poole; and the others covered work on the stately area of Edinburgh New Town and a modest revolving fund scheme in Fife. Each project required heavy financing and each was centred around a concentration of historic buildings.

The Trust's third aim was the launch of a revolving fund for historic buildings. The Architectural Heritage Fund was the result, the Government matching pound for pound the sums raised from other sources. The Fund survives as a lasting memorial to EAHY and has been the inspiration of other funds set up on the same model.

Designated years are now so commonplace that it is difficult to assess their effectiveness, but it is hard to grudge EAHY credit for raising the level of public awareness. The energetic chairmanship of Lady Dartmouth ensured that the Year was true to its theme of relating the heritage to non-outstanding areas, and the Architectural Heritage Fund ensured that its good work would be continued. Much credit for the success of the year belongs to the Civic Trust, who acted as the secretariat (one of the few non-Government secretariats in Europe). Long after the last glittering reception in St James's Palace that closed the Year its slogan, 'A Future for the Past', lived on. It was all part of raising public awareness about the heritage and about what ordinary citizens could do to help preserve it.

3.5
Conservation after EAHY

The critics would have it otherwise of course.They pointed out that during its first six months for every day of European Architectural Heritage Year, a listed building was demolished. Quite apart from the fact that this overlooked what listing was all about – as a register of the best architecture, not an absolute bar on its demolition – this ignored the significant victories that the conservationists won. When a row of very good but unspectacular Victorian houses in Kensington was saved in 1975, it was a victory for conservation over the plans of the Royal College of Art to replace them with a new building very much in the idiom of the 70s, and when in 1976 the Courts upheld the Secretary of State's duty (as opposed to a discretionary power) to list, that too was confirmation of the conservationists' cause (the picturesquely named case of *Amalgamated Investment and Property Co.* v. *Walker (John) and Sons*). The pressure from the developers might be growing, but this was a high water mark for conservationists. They were never to have things quite so much their way again. For the planner and the developer, it seemed that the threat of listing, or of being affected by a conservation area designation, had never been stronger. The tide would flow their way, and the efforts of conservationists would be to some extent frustrated by new stringencies in local government finance; but that time was not quite yet, and in the mid-1970s it seemed as if conservationists would find their advance unimpeded.

There was one further legislative advance for the conservationists. This was the Ancient Monuments & Archaeological Areas Act 1979. This brought forward existing monuments legislation, and introduced a new provision for the designation of 'areas of archaeological importance' in which rescue digs could precede the redevelopment of a site. Here was a possible solution to a problem sometimes found when digging foundations for new buildings in old historic centres, where excavation could reveal remains of archaeological importance. The new Act was almost the first weapon that had been given specifically to the archaeologists. To some developers it must have seemed like a further attempt to stymie their activities, although the first areas of archaeological importance were not designated until 1984.

There was now, however, a feeling in some quarters that the pendulum might have swung too far the conservationists' way. In particular, the practice of spot-listing – literally adding buildings to the list on the spot – was a danger that developers, especially in urban centres, had come to fear. The value of a city centre site could plummet overnight if the buildings on it were listed, since the expectation of redevelopment being allowed was considerably reduced. The system seemed unfair because there was no mechanism for the developer to ascertain the position before they invested time and money in the project; while the Secretary of State, as the Johnny Walker case had shown, had no option in law but to list if it was concluded that the building in question had the necessary special architectural or historic interest.

The result was the introduction of the certificate of immunity from listing. The Local Government, Planning & Land Act 1980 inserted a new section in the 1971 Act enabling developers (or anyone else for that matter) to apply to the Secretary of State for a certificate stating that he would not list the building in question for at least a period of five years from the date of its issue. The application was a double-edged sword in that the Secretary of State, having had his attention drawn to the building, might conclude that it did possess special architectural or historic interest and spot-list it; but at least developers could now get the listing question settled at an early stage. If they chose to press ahead with their plans and then found that the building was spot-listed, they would have no-one to blame but themselves for having neglected to apply for a certificate.

The certificate of immunity procedure was certainly not anti-conservationist: indeed it has helped to remove one of the unfortunate occasional consequences of spot-listing without undermining the statutory duty to list; and in so doing has improved the credibility of the listing system. It formed part of a package of measures in the 1980 Act that made minor adjustments to the listing system and to listed building control in the light of experience. Specifically, the Act also

1. extended statutory protection not only to features of special architectural or historic interest but also to their setting;
2. amended the listed building and conservation area consent procedures by always requiring a consent application to be made

separately from one for planning permission;

3. introduced time limits on listed building consents;

4. brought in a right to apply for the retention of unauthorized works (which did not however stop it being an offence to carry out work to a listed building without first applying for consent).

3.6
The national resurvey of historic buildings

Developers' worries about undue pressure from the conservation lobby were not only caused by the growth in public awareness and sympathy for the conservationists' case: they were also caused by the sheer growth in the numbers of listed buildings. When the first survey of historic buildings had been completed in the the late 1960s, they were 120 000 listed buildings in England, but the lists were already largely out of date. Many had been compiled 10 or 20 years previously, and the permissive system of control that existed before 1968 meant that many buildings had long disappeared or had been altered or extended in such a way that they were no longer of listable quality. Coverage, although nominally comprehensive, had been patchy in some areas, particularly in the countryside. The lists also reflected the architectural tastes, by and large, of 20 years before and made few forays into listing buildings of later than early nienteenth century date. There had been, as we saw in the last chapter, a resurgence of interest in Victorian architecture from the late 1950s onwards, while architectural scholarship had itself moved on and needed to be reflected in the lists.

Hence, in 1969 the Ministry of Housing and Local Government took a deep breath and launched a national resurvey of historic buildings. It must have seemed like painting the Forth Bridge – no sooner completed than needing to be started again – and was something of a courageous step by Government. This time, the investigators were given a new set of criteria which had the approval of the HBC. These ensured that Victorian architecture was to be included in the new exercise, and that the investigators were to consider not only date but also the economic, social or technological significance of the building and its importance as an example of its building-type. The criteria, which were approved by the HBC in March 1970 are still the basis for selection today (Appendix A), and the only amendments that have been made to them cover the listing of inter-war buildings and most recently the listing of a few selected post-war buildings.

There was one further significant change. The new resurvey lists dropped the old non-statutory Grade III buildings (although most on resurvey have been found to be worth upgrading to II). So the statutory lists really were now statutory lists. Out too went the badly-duplicated dog-eared sheets of foolscap in favour of neat volumes comb-bound in green covers which soon won them the name of greenbacks which has stuck ever since. The old 'provisional' and 'statutory' lists were abolished in favour of the single volume: the rather redundant attempt to list the owners and occupiers of each building included was scrapped and new descriptions incorporating addresses, grid references and a fuller description of the building were substituted. The new lists were a great improvement on their predecessors. The question was how long it would take to cover the whole country again.

The problem was that no-one seems to have set a planned timescale. Nor was there any certainty that the staff resources for the resurvey would be made available – especially on a timetable that seemed likely to embrace two or three different administrations, each with their competing priorities. Precedence was given in the opening years of the resurvey to the historic centres, but even here the scheduling of work was not always straightforward. Bath had its new list in 1972, but Westminster, largely because it was such a huge historic centre, had to wait until 1987. Progress was slow and the pressure from active conservationists (not to mention intending developers) was growing, and so a lot of the investigators' efforts were directed at the time-consuming process of spot-listing, which meant they were not able to get on with their resurvey work as expeditiously as they would have wished.

The national resurvey proceeded slowly through the 1970s. The Department's investigators were now full-time and well-qualified – the whiff of the gentleman and lady amateur that had bedevilled the first years of the first survey was finally expelled. In order to keep the lists abreast of public taste, the HBC also commissioned Sir Nikolaus Pevsner, who was one of its members, to draw up a first selection of inter-war buildings that might be added to the lists. This he did, and although the selection bore all the eclecticism of his *Buildings of England* series, it was at least a step in the right direction. It is something of a sign of the times that inter-war architecture, which had been ignored at the outset of the resurvey, should now be included in the lists only a few years later. The protection of the best architecture of the 20s and 30s did not stop there. Further additions were made by way of spot-lists: the Midland Hotel in Morecambe, for instance, with its fine bas-relief sculpture by Eric Gill, was graded II* – the second highest order of listing – when the 'Pevsner 50', which included buildings of such international standing as the Delawarr Pavilion at Bexhill-on-Sea by Mendelsohn and Chermayeff, were only listed Grade II (in the case of the Delawarr Pavilion at least, this grading has now been rightly raised to II*).

The problem was that all this was proceeding at such a slow pace and that staff cuts were making the position worse. In 1974 there had been18 investigators; by 1981, these had been reduced to just four. The Department was by this time barely able to keep up with spot-listing requests, let alone the resurvey work. And then there was Firestone.

The Firestone factory on the Great West Road in London was one of those art deco confections which sprung up along the arterial roads leading out of the capital between the wars. Designed in1928 by the Wallis, Gilbert partnership (whose finest work was the glorious Hoover factory in Perivale), it was closed in the summer of 1980 by the Firestone company, who began to negotiate its sale to a subsidiary of the multinational company, Trafalgar House. The newly-formed Thirties Society wrote to the Department of the Environment in July asking for the factory to be spot-listed. In August an investigator visited the site in response to an alert from the local planning authority, and papers were prepared for spot-listing. On August Bank holiday weekend the papers were ready and would have been signed in the normal course of events the following week but, on the Saturday, the bulldozers moved in. They began by demolishing the centre of the facade, architecturally the most interesting portion of the building, leaving the less interesting pavilions at either end till last. A more cynical act of demolition was difficult to imagine.

What was more surprising, however, was the public reaction. The Firestone factory had been a prominent feature on one of London's main roads. It was a large and handsome building in a stripped 1930s classical style, and it had clearly won much public affection. Trafalgar House's methods were not designed to win public support and they did not do so: there was an editorial in the *Daily Telegraph* and the Secretary of State, Michael Heseltine, was moved to take action.

In fact, the Firestone factory could have been saved by the local planning authority, Hounslow London Borough Council, serving a

Grade II listed buildings: *top*: vernacular 16th century house in Suffolk; and *bottom*: a pub in Harlington, Bedfordshire.

building preservation notice. But they were probably aware that the Department had spot-listing in mind and, if their notice had failed to be confirmed, they stood the risk of being liable for compensation. For its part, the Department could, and no doubt would, have acted more swiftly had it known of the imminence of the threat but the demolition people had acted completely within the law. What the Firestone incident demonstrated was that spot-listing is no substitute for a comprehensive resurvey list and at the present rate of progress nationwide coverage seemed unlikely before the millenium.

The lesson was quickly taken by Michael Heseltine. He ordered a speeding-up, and the national resurvey became the accelerated national resurvey. In order to supplement the work of his own investigators, help was secured from both the public and private sectors. In phase 1 of the accelerated resurvey, 22 selected local authorities prepared draft lists on a repayment basis under the supervision of the Department's own expert staff. There was a precedent for this in the 1970s, when the Greater London Council had carried out fieldwork in some of the London Boroughs, using some of the excellent staff in their Historic Buildings Division. More radical than the use of local authority staff was the employment in phase 2 of the resurvey of 11 private sector architectural practices to carry out fieldwork, again under the supervision of the Department. Clearly there was a need to establish a uniformity of standards across the country and, with so many fieldworkers and so many different types of architecture to deal with, this was not easy. The original plan was that fieldwork for the resurvey should finish in 1990. In fact, it ended in all but a few areas in May 1987, a great tribute to the energy, enthusiasm and skill of all those involved.

It is no exaggeration to say that Firestone was a sacrificial lamb. Out of the shock and outrage that followed its demolition, there followed a new determination that such an incident should never be allowed to happen again. It has, of course. The spot-listing process has remained an adjunct to the resurvey and occasionally it has failed to work in time to save a building of worth. The new impetus Firestone gave to the resurvey, however, has ensured that such instances have been rare.

What has been even more encouraging is that the resurvey and the list reviews that are still going on have had such wide public support and acceptance. We have mentioned before the English-person's tendency to cherish their property rights. Listed building control, like the planning system, can be seen as the heavy hand of the state descending and restricting those rights in an arbitrary and unfair way. Remarkably few owners have seen it that way. Rather, there has been a pride of ownership that sees listing – rightly – as an accolade, a recognition that the property is a recognized part of the national heritage. The co-operation of owners has been vital in the progress of the fieldwork. In order to assess most properties, it is not sufficient to inspect them from the street: the fieldworker will need to ensure that the building is complete and unaltered, and in most instances this will involve an internal inspection. It is rare for this to be refused, and it is worth stating here that although fieldworkers do have a statutory right of entry (which is exercised through a rather cumbersome process of serving notice) not once in the course of the resurvey did this right need to be enforced.

There was some concern about the conduct of a tiny minority of fieldworkers, whose enthusiasm exceeded their tact on occasion, and about the absence of any statutory right of appeal against listing. This surfaced in the course of debates in the Commons and more particularly the Lords on the Housing & Planning Bill in1986. Specifically, there were moves to introduce a right of appeal and to effect a form of provisional listing similar to the procedure for building preservation notices. The Minister responsible, Lord Skelmersdale, pointed out in the course of debate that of the 23000 buildings added to the list in the previous year, only three dozen had been the subject of representations to the Department. A full-blown appeals mechanism was hardly necessary for such a tiny number of cases, and the Department preferred instead to rely on an informal procedure to consider representations about why a building should not be added to the list; indeed, it argued that an informal avenue is more attractive to owners who might find form-filling and the complexities of inquiries procedure off-putting. Parliament accepted the Minister's argument, and the system remained intact, but the Department did agree to give more publicity and guidance to the informal appeals mechanism, and to issue a formal code of conduct for fieldworkers.

The numbers of listed buildings rose from 120000 in 1970 to 273000 by the end of 1980. With the results of the national resurvey's acceleration becoming evident, this figure rose to 395000 by the end of 1987 and in 1994 stood at 500000. As a proportion of the nation's total building stock, this means that 0.7% of buildings were listed in 1970 (about 1 building in 140): this figure rose to 2%

(1 in 50) by 1987 and now stands at $2\frac{1}{4}$% (1 in 43). What the figures do not bring out are the advances in architectural scholarship that have been brought about by the resurvey itself. Our knowledge of vernacular architecture, almost untouched in the first survey, has grown enormously as we have painstakingly surveyed what actually exists in this country. The lists have had to cope too with other improvements in architectural scholarship which mean occasionally looking back over covered ground again: the Arts and Crafts architecture of the late nineteenth century is one such field where research and changing tastes have accorded a new importance to a rather neglected field. These trends have defied the intention of those who began the resurvey that the new lists should be in any way definitive. They have become instead rather more organic, with additions and revisions reflecting the wider world of architectural scholarship and research.

3.7
The foundation of English Heritage

Quite apart from the lists, however, by far the most important development of the 1980s was the establishment of the Historic Buildings and Monuments Commission for England, known to everyone as English Heritage. The moving force behind the new body was again Michael Heseltine. The Directorate of Ancient Monuments and Historic Buildings always sat rather oddly in the Department of the Environment because so much of its work was executive in nature – the care and maintenance of ancient monuments and those other historic properties that were in the ownership of the Department. The Department's other main executive arm, dealing with the Government estate, had long been hived off into the Property Services Agency, albeit retaining its links with the Department. On top of this, there was a strong argument for saying that England's monuments would be better marketed by a free-standing agency than by civil servants; and there was also the point that an independent Commission could comment more freely on behalf of conservation than a Directorate that was tied to the Secretary of State and thus unable to take any other side in a dispute.

All these arguments were canvassed in a consultation document from the Department (*The Way Forward*); this was followed by the necessary legislation in the National Heritage Act 1983 and the

Commission was established on 1 April 1984. It took with it those technical staff who looked after the Department's monuments (but not the Royal palaces), the monuments themselves and some of the administrative staff. It left behind a body of officials to advise the Secretary of State on conservation questions and who were responsible for making decisions on his behalf on the listing of historic buildings and the scheduling of ancient monuments. No decision-making powers were delegated to the Commission except in relation to grants, but the National Heritage Act 1983 made the Commission the Secretary of State's statutory advisers on a range of historic buildings and ancient monuments matters. The Historic Buildings Council for England and the Ancient Monuments Board were wound up, but the Commission adopted its own committee structure to ensure it still had access to expert outside advice in presenting its views to the Secretary of State.

The Commission was also empowered under the 1983 Act to compile its own register of historic gardens, which it has done along the same lines as the lists of historic buildings (except that it has adopted a county-by-county basis). In addition, the Commission acquired a new block of work when the Greater London Council was abolished in 1986. It took over the GLC's functions with respect to the London Boroughs, as well as the staff of its Historic Buildings Division (which means that, among other things, the Commission is now responsible for the 'Blue Plaque' scheme).

The Commission's main efforts have been towards public education and the monuments that it manages on behalf of the Secretary of State. The Commission has done much good work in promoting conservation among a wider public and in encouraging that public to participate in the upkeep of the built heritage both through gate receipts at the monuments it manages and through membership of English Heritage itself.

The Historic Buildings and Monuments Commission for England has no exact parallel in the other parts of the United Kingdom. In Scotland, responsibility for built heritage matters is vested in Historic Scotland, an agency of the Scottish Development Department. In Wales, all heritage functions are handled by CADW (which is the Welsh verb 'to keep'), operating as part of the Welsh Office. In Northern Ireland, the separate Department of the Environment (Northern Ireland), which is answerable to the Secretary of State for Northern Ireland, continues to be responsible for heritage affairs. In Scotland, there were 41 000 listed buildings at the beginning of 1995, in Wales 17 000 and in Northern Ireland 8600.

3.8
Developments since 1986

The Housing & Planning Act 1986 did contain some measures adjusting listed building control, most notably in respect of the defence available to those demolishing a building without consent in cases where a dangerous structure is involved. In 1987 the Department issued a new circular (8/87) consolidating all previous advice on conservation matters and amending some of the Secretary of State's directions. This habit of consolidating advice had been started in 1977, and the issue of a fresh consolidating circular was welcome to most planning officers. Historic building and conservation area legislation was consolidated into the Planning (Listed Buildings & Conservation Areas) Act 1990, which came into force on 24 August 1990.

In the late 1980s, international pressures began to play a more important part in the UK conservation scene. The UK had ratified in 1984 the World Heritage Convention, which had been adopted by UNESCO 12 years earlier. The Convention required a World Heritage List to be established, with individual governments nominating the sites.Ten such sites have been nominated in England, including Stonehenge, Blenheim Palace and the Tower of London. No additional controls apply to these places (they would hardly be necessary) but the fact of their being on the World Heritage List is a reinforcing factor in their protection.

Perhaps the most singular episode of this period was the Department's programme to list a selection of the familiar red telephone kiosks that were being replaced by British Telecom. These became the focus of a lobbying campaign directed at both the Department and BT. The first kiosks were listed in August 1986 and were unusual early designs from the 1920s and early 1930s. The real spate of listing took place once the Department had accepted the Thirty Year Rule for listing (of which more in a moment). At that stage, many thousands more kiosks became eligible for listing, and the Department and English Heritage have had to enforce the criterion of special architectural or historic interest very strictly, using the setting of the kiosk, and in particular its relationship to other listed buildings nearby as its guide. As a result, well over 1000 kiosks have been listed to date.

After the Firestone incident, the Department produced criteria for listing inter-war buildings, but the end-date for listing remained 1939. No building designed after that date was considered for listing, since it was felt to be difficult to obtain the necessary degree of perspective on its age to assess its special interest. There was certainly a logic in this, and it meant that the Department was effectively operating a Thirty Year Rule, as the resurvey had begun in 1969 and there were good arguments for keeping the listing criteria as standard as possible throughout the fieldwork. In Scotland, however, there had long been a rolling Thirty Year Rule, which meant that the end-date for listing was brought forward annually. When the Brynmawr Rubber Factory in Wales was listed (it had been designed in 1953), the pressure on the English became harder to bear, particularly as the resurvey neared its close. The difficulty lay in what should be listed. Modern architecture is a difficult area. Much of it is regarded as a failure and while public affection for the Royal Festival Hall or the 'prefab' might be strong, it in no way commands the popular support of the best architecture of the 20s and 30s. The Department decided to adopt an imaginative solution. In March 1987, it announced that it would adopt the Thirty Year Rule and that as a curtain-raiser there would be public competition to identify the first tranche of candidates. The Department, however, went one better than the Scots and the Welsh: it agreed to list outstanding buildings between 10 and 30 years old provided that there was an immediate threat to them.

The first modern building was listed ahead of the competition because of the threat of redevelopment. This was Sir Alfred Richardson's Bracken House, the *Financial Times* building in central London, which was listed in August 1988. Following the competition, and with the agreement of English Heritage, 18 further post-war buildings were added to the list, among them the Royal Festival Hall, Coventry Cathedral and the Stockwell Bus Garage. There are now around 100 listed modern buildings, including at least one 1970s building (the Willis Faber offices in Ipswich by Foster Associates, 1975) listed Grade I.

The most significant change in the period was the creation in April 1992 of a new Department of National Heritage (DNH). Among its new responsibilities the Department took charge of built conservation from the Department of the Environment (DoE), leaving the latter however with those listed building and conservation area consent cases which were called in or fell to the Secretary of State to decide, together with appeal casework and some related matters (see Chapter 4). The new DNH took over the sponsorship of English Heritage. It also took over the former DoE staff, ensuring some welcome continuity. They are now a unit in a Department dedicated to promoting the heritage in the widest sense and, because the Department is smaller, their voice is more easily heard.

DNH's main achievements have been twofold. First, they have completed the editing and publication of the national resurvey lists, so completing the exercise begun in 1969. But there has been no sea change in public taste since that date requiring a third exercise. Instead, the Department and English Heritage are revising just a few lists from the early years of the resurvey. More significantly, they are also looking at building types which are thought to be under-represented in the lists. Second, DNH has continued the revision and consolidation of the conservation advice that is issued to local planning authorities and developers. In November 1990, the DoE issued a Planning Policy Guidance Note on *Archaeology & Planning* (PPG16). DNH followed this up in September 1994 with the issue of a further PPG on *Planning & the Historic Environment* (PPG15). This updates and supersedes the policy advice in Circular 8/87. As well as revising the listing and listed building control criteria, the circular stressed the Government's new emphasis on establishing a framework for developers through the development plan system, and introduced new and helpful advice on curtilage controls and fixtures, and on transport and traffic management issues. The circular highlights the importance of conserving the built environment in the context of sustainable development.

All this is a long way from the early days of the resurvey. What is certain however is that Britain's lists of buildings of special architectural or historic interest are the most comprehensive in the western world, and are backed up by a strong framework of statutory controls. The dedication and care that has gone into the preparation of the lists and into policing the controls offers good hope for the future of the heritage in this country. The question now is what we should do with the heritage we have so carefully chronicled and protected. That is a question to which we shall turn again in the last chapter.

Chapter 4

THE MAIN
PLAYERS

Conservation in Britain is only possible at all because of the joint
action of public, private and voluntary sector agencies. If that
sounds like a cliché, it is nonetheless important for that. In broad
terms, central Government provides the framework for conservation – the lists of historic buildings, the schedules of ancient
monuments and the controls that regulate them and conservation
areas – while English Heritage and the voluntary groups provide the
expertise and in many cases the actual physical labour that keeps
the heritage together. The local authorities bring the work of central Government and the voluntary groups together, decide the
majority of consent cases and work to protect and enhance the
heritage of their local communities.

This of course is the ideal. In reality, there are some local authorities that are not as caring towards their local heritage as they
should be – especially the buildings for which they themselves are
responsible – while a few amenity societies can sometimes behave
as if it were immoral to remove a single brick or stone from a listed
structure or to construct a new building of any kind in a historic
area. There is also the question of cash, some of which is provided
by all the agencies and groups we have mentioned but not always in
a way that the others think right or just.

This question of balance – of whether each agency is doing
enough and whether it is even doing the right thing – is one of the
wellsprings of debate in the conservation movement. At best, it
means there is a creative tension between the agencies and a good
and constructive measure of cooperation between them. At worst,
it can lead, unfortunately, to bickering and recrimination that is not
in the best interests of conservation as a whole.

We shall look in turn at the main players in the conservation movement. We shall deal with the formally-constituted bodies, but we should remember that their work would be a great deal more difficult were it not for the efforts of private individuals and companies who give freely of their time and their money to help preserve the heritage. Without them, and the climate of acceptance that they have created for conservation, the framework of control would not work so well, and the voluntary agencies and English Heritage would be ploughing on pretty stony ground.

4.1
The Department of the Environment

The Department of the Environment (DoE) is a strange creation. It was founded in 1970 when super-Ministries were fashionable and its first Secretary of State was Peter Walker, a young Tory technocrat who brought considerable impetus to the new Department. It brought together the Ministries of Housing and Local Government, Public Building and Works and Transport. It was a slightly odd collection – particularly the inclusion of Transport – but it seemed at the time to represent the holistic attitude to planning which underlay the Town & Country Planning Acts and most particularly the 1968 Act with its new structure plan provisions which touched on transport and even economic planning as well as the more familiar elements of development control.

From the point of view of conservation, the new Department certainly seemed worthwhile. As we have seen, there was in the 1960s, if not before, an increasing realization that conservation was part and parcel of the mainstream planning system and not simply a slightly esoteric and specialist subject of interest to only a few planners in a few heritage centres. In particular, the change of attitudes typified in *Preservation and Change* could be given effect only if conservation was given an equal voice not just with land-use planners but also with the transport planners who would now all be in the same Department.

And so it proved to be. There was no overnight revolution that put conservation top of the heap in the Department's priorities. But at least the conservation planners within the Department were now able to talk to their road and strategic planning colleagues on an equal footing; to involve themselves where necessary in the formative stages of project planning; and to make their views known before proposals went to Departmental Ministers for approval.

The key unit in this was the Directorate of Ancient Monuments and Historic Buildings (DAMHB), known to all as 'Damby' (and occasionally to its detractors as 'Damn B's). The Directorate was headed by an Under-secretary – third in the pecking order of senior civil servants – and consisted of a large executive arm which was responsible for the maintenance of the royal palaces and those ancient monuments in the Government's ownership or guardianship, as well as for advising on grant applications; and a much smaller corps of branches listing buildings and carrying out the classic and traditional functions of advising Ministers on the policy aspects of handling individual cases. The Directorate included one particularly valuable branch which combined the skills of architects and planners: the Historic Areas Conservation branch. This was able to make a direct and valuable contribution to the Department's assessment of the structure and other local plans that were coming in, as well as advising on a range of other matters, not least the road plans of their new Departmental colleagues on the Transport side.

Another key component was the Department's network of Regional Offices. These replicated the integrated approach at local level, with the Regional Director – again an Under-secretary – providing the focus for balancing conservation and other interests. The Regional Offices had an executive rather than a policy role on the conservation side, since their prime interest lay in casework affecting listed buildings, and later conservation areas. But since their regional planners were in the front line in taking the new structure plans through their tortuous procedural paths to adoption – and were in touch with DAMHB among others in doing this – the policy element was not lacking. Curiously, even though the Departments of the Environment and Transport have now been split, the integrated Government Offices in the Regions permit this cross-Departmental working to continue. This is a happy recognition that transport is central to development planning – and of course vice versa.

The corporate style of Ted Heath's administration lasted until the mid-70s. In 1976, a separate Department of Transport was established with its own Secretary of State, although the links with Environment remained strong, especially in the Regional Offices. A rather more radical move, as we shall see, was the removal of most of the executive functions of the DAMHB to the new quango English Heritage in 1984. This left the Department as almost wholly a policy-making body, setting the scene and the pace for others – English Heritage, the local authorities and the other statutory and voluntary agencies.

The creation of the Department of National Heritage (DNH) in 1992 stripped the DoE of most of its remaining heritage work. The Heritage and Royal Estate directorate that had replaced DAMHB went across almost completely to the new Department, leaving the DoE and its regional offices with essentially only listed building and conservation area casework and appeals, since these were so closely bound up with the general development control system for which the DoE is responsible. In practice, the two Departments work closely together, but it is worth recalling that there are two Secretaries of State interested in conservation – broadly, National Heritage setting the policy and Environment dealing with the casework.

4.2
The Department of National Heritage

DNH's conservation responsibilities are carried out by its Heritage Directorate, headed by an Under-secretary. The Department is charged with:

1. policy on archaeology and the conservation of the built heritage;
2. sponsorship of English Heritage, the National Heritage Memorial Fund, the Royal Commission on Historical Monuments, the Royal Fine Arts Commission and other heritage public bodies;
3. listing and scheduling and scheduled monument consents;
4. casework on repairs notices and associated compulsory purchase orders; policy procedures and reserve powers on the designation of conservation areas;
5. grants to heritage bodies;
6. the ecclesiastical exemption from listed building control.

The Heritage & Tourism Group of DNH is staffed by administrative civil servants who rely in turn on English Heritage for professional advice. But like all civil servants, including their opposite numbers in the DoE, their decisions are only taken in the name of the Secretary of State (and we ourselves in the chapters to follow will speak of the Secretary of State when in fact we will often be speaking of his Department, which acts in his name). The Secretary of State will personally be involved in a few controversial decisions; others will be taken by one of his immediate Ministerial subordinates (sometimes called junior Ministers) at Minister of State and Parliamentary Under-secretary of State level. They will have day-to-day responsibility for heritage matters, including answering the sizeable postbag that comes from MPs and members of the House of Lords; and answering parliamentary questions on heritage subjects.

4.3
English Heritage

The Government first floated the idea of a separate executive agency for the heritage in a paper entitled *Organisation of Ancient Monuments and Historic Buildings in England* in November 1981. It invited comments on the proposal, and these were given a firm foundation in *The Way Forward*, published in 1982. This set out the Government's view on the case for change, and the arguments against. It concluded that a new body should be created, and it cited in its favour the arguments that:

1. the expert professionalism required in the heritage field meant that the work was suitable to be carried out by an agency at arm's length from Government;
2. there would be 'positive and creative' advantages in bringing together diffuse and dispersed arrangements into a single body;
3. there would be an opportunity to apply a new approach to presentation and marketing;
4. the new body should be able to harness the 'abundant goodwill' in the heritage field, through both private donations and voluntary assistance.

In short, the new heritage body would be very much in line with the Government's general aim to reduce the functions of Government departments where those functions could be more effectively carried out elsewhere.

The new creation, the Historic Buildings and Monuments Commission for England, required legislation. The National Heritage Act 1983 allowed the Commission to be established, and it began functioning on 1 April 1984. Since its formal name was such a mouthful, it quickly became known as English Heritage, despite the Government's refusal in *The Way Forward* to countenance the use of the word heritage in the new body's title. The new organization had seven functions.

1. As the Secretary of State's statutory adviser on the scheduling of ancient monuments and in the granting of scheduled monument consent; and on the listing of buildings of special architectural or historic interest and the granting of listed building consent; as well as on more general heritage matters. We shall see in ensuing chapters how this role has been translated into the legislation, giving English Heritage a powerful voice.

2. The Commission was given the Secretary of State's curatorial role over ancient monuments, both those in his ownership and those over which he exercised powers of guardianship (see Chapter 8). This linked in neatly with:

3. The Commission was created partly in order to improve the presentation of England's ancient monuments. The DoE had never won high marks for its marketing, and the new body was intended to attract more visitors both to enhance its own income and to encourage a greater awareness of the nation's heritage. The aim was not to create a Disneyworld, but to show that the heritage was an attractive and interesting subject with many places of interest to visit. The success of the National Trust was a sign of what could be achieved in this field.

4. The Commission had an executive function in administering those historic buildings and conservation area grants that were previously handed out by the Secretary of State. This was a topic where the staff who now found themselves in the Commission had always been closely involved both in advising on individual applications and in helping to work up schemes for whole areas.

5. The former DAMHB had always had a strong commitment to archaeology, and this was transferred to the Commission. Rescue archaeology has become a subject of growing importance, and the Commission's interest in it has been particularly strong.

6. No-one had previously brought together the interests of the conservation movement outside Government. The Commission was

never intended to supersede the work of the voluntary conservation and amenity societies, but it could co-ordinate their efforts around specific projects or in lobbying Government. Just as importantly, by having a system of individual membership, it could tap the growing fund of public goodwill for conservation and use it for practical help in protecting and enhancing the environment.

7. The Commission had a number of other miscellaneous powers – for instance, the construction of a national register of historic gardens which acquire a statutory status with the introduction of consultation requirements for planning applications affecting Grade I and II* parks and gardens on the register.

Some felt that the Government should have gone further in giving the Commission an executive power in listing and ancient monuments work, instead of restricting it to an advisory role. The reason for this is not hard to find. Decisions in such cases are often contentious, and it is surely right that Ministers should be answerable to Parliament for the decisions that they and their officials take. Quangos are answerable to no-one and, short of winding it up, axing its grant or sacking the Commissioners, there is no formal mechanism of control over English Heritage any more than there is for most other such bodies. Listing in particular is sometimes felt to trespass on property rights, and it would be difficult to take decisions out of the political sphere. In the matter of casework on consents, it would be inconsistent to take responsibility out of Ministers' hands, since the present systems are so closely tied in with normal development control where the Secretary of State for the Environment enjoys parallel powers for serious or contentious cases. The issue was addressed in setting the Commission up, and again in 1986 when English Heritage raised the issue in their evidence to the House of Commons Select Committee inquiry into the heritage. On both occasions, the Government concluded that the present arrangements should remain, and it must be added that there has been little pressure for any change.

The only modification that has been made to the Commission's list of functions since its inception has been the addition of the Greater London Council's functions (and staff) when the GLC was wound up. This has given the Commission some executive responsibilities in London as well as care of the former GLC Historic Buildings Division with its reputation as a centre of scholarship on the architecture of the capital.

By general consent, the Commission has performed very well since its foundation. As the statutory adviser to the Secretary of State, its experts have continued to enjoy a high standing, but their independence from the Department has given them a new authority. The presentation and marketing of the heritage has been particularly successful and special efforts have been made to bring the heritage to the attention of schoolchildren. Government, for its part, has responded to English Heritage's new tasks with large tranches of grant-aid: £104.1m in 1994/95, rising to £105.8m in each of the three following years.

English Heritage is now a valuable potential ally for any developer or anyone opposing a development. It is sometimes possible to discuss with the Commission the sort of proposals that are being contemplated and to secure an informal view from them in a way that would not be possible with the Secretary of State for the Environment because of his quasi-judicial role on call-in or appeal. The fact that English Heritage has developed a large regional structure – that is to say with a network of casework officers – is also helping it to establish its credibility. True, its committee structure, stemming from the Commissioners themselves and leading through a host of committees and sub-committees, sometimes seems complicated, but these largely bring together into one organization the various boards and committees that formerly existed in the DoE with the addition of one or two others to take account of the new organization and the functions taken over from the GLC. English Heritage has now put itself firmly on the conservation map.

4.4
Arrangements in Scotland, Wales and Northern Ireland

We have already outlined in section 3.7 the arrangements that are current in the other parts of the United Kingdom. In Wales and in Scotland responsibility for the heritage is vested in CADW and Historic Scotland, respectively. In Northern Ireland, there is centralized structure under the DoE (Northern Ireland).

But although the administrative structures differ, the legal provisions throughout the United Kingdom are broadly the same. We shall thus continue to refer to the Secretary of State, although this

Top: Eighteenth century building swallowed up by suburbia and protected by listing. *Below*: A war memorial – humble enough, but listed for its historical association with the First World War.

may mean the one for the Environment or National Heritage (in England) and those for Scotland, Wales and Northern Ireland in their own countries. We shall also refer to the Commission, although this may be taken to mean Historic Scotland, CADW and the DoE (Northern Ireland), as well as English Heritage.

4.5
The Royal Commissions on Historical Monuments

There are separate Royal Commissions on Historical Monuments (RCHM) (to give them their more manageable titles) for England, Scotland and Wales. Their function is essentially that of national archives of the built heritage. As we saw in Chapter 2, the English RCHM was established to provide inventories of buildings in each county: the painstaking work was not speedy enough to be effective for planning purposes, and it was partly in response to this that the statutory lists were begun. But the National Monuments Record, which includes elaborate photographic records of buildings which have long since disappeared (as well as many thousands which are happily still standing) is a unique creation. The archive is given statutory backing by the requirement to notify the Royal Commission of listed building consent applications for demolition and the requirement not to demolish a listed building, even after consent is granted, until the Royal Commission has had an opportunity to record it.

The Royal Commission, however, is not simply a repository of information. It is itself actively engaged on archaeological work, and it also publishes the information it contains in a series of attractively presented books. The fact that the National Monument Record is photographic as well as written helps the Royal Commission greatly in this respect. It has a treasure-house of information about the national architectural heritage, and it deserves to be considered by a wider audience.

At the time the Historic Buildings and Monuments Commission was created, the Government did consider whether the older Royal Commission should be subsumed within it. The general conclusion was that there would be no benefit from this. The archival role of the Royal Commission is rather different from the pro-active campaigning role of the Commission, and there is little overlap between them. Working relations are understandably close, and it is difficult

to see that there would be any increase in the so-called three E's –
economy, efficiency and effectiveness – by a merger. Nor would
there seem to be anything to be gained by bringing together the
three territorial Royal Commissions into one body. The position
was reviewed in 1987, and the same conclusions were reached. So
the present arrangements, with Government grant-aiding their
work, seem set to continue.

4.6
Local authorities

Local authorities are in the front line of conservation. More than
any other individual body or agency, their actions determine the
fate of the heritage in their areas. They have a battery of powers
which can be deployed for good or ill. They determine not only the
fate of those buildings for which there are planning applications or
moves to obtain listed building or conservation area consent, but
also possess powers to grant-aid those buildings and to improve the
quality of the localities in which they are situated.

This is just as Parliament intended. After all, the very core of the
listing legislation – section 1 of the 1990 Act – states that the lists
are produced for the guidance of local planning authorities in the per-
formance of their functions. The Secretary of State compiles the
lists, but then he hands them over to the planning authority and says
effectively 'Do what you will with them'. It is the planning authority that usually decides when listed building consent will be granted,
and if so on what terms; it is the planning authority that decides
when a repairs notice will be served on a listed building in a state of
dilapidation, and it is the planning authority that decides when to
proceed to compulsory purchase. In the case of conservation areas, it
is the local planning authority that is both responsible for designation and for the granting of conservation area consent for demolition.
There are certainly opportunities for the Secretary of State to inter-
vene (and there are more of them than in the general run of planning
cases), and he will also act as the deciding authority in the case of
appeals. It is the planning authority, however, that stands as the first
line of defence in conserving the heritage in its area.

This arrangement simply builds on the position that applies in
normal development control – the run of the mill planning applications. Since many if not most applications for listed building

consent are accompanied by planning applications, such an arrangement is only sensible. But of course the workload has grown considerably since 1968 when, as we have seen, the present system of listed building control was established. The DoE has not kept a year-by-year record of the numbers of consent applications since 1968, but the increase in the numbers of listed buildings have told their own tale. Much of the increase in planning authorities' workload on the conservation front has been at a time when their expenditure has been under severe constraint; and it is a tribute to them that for the most part the issue of the new and very much expanded resurvey lists has been welcomed by them despite the accompanying increase in their workload. Certainly the definitive nature of the lists, which should avoid for the most part the need to take urgent and administratively expensive action to protect buildings of note, should be welcome: and certainly too the Government has done its best to keep the extra burden on authorities to a minimum, as we shall see. At the end of the day, however, most authorities have been co-operative in taking on board an enhanced workload both for their staff and for their elected members.

Most of this burden has been shouldered by the second tier district or borough councils. They are the planning authorities for the purposes of most conservation legislation (and indeed for other forms of development control), although county councils, where they continue to exist, do have a concurrent power to designate conservation areas (but only after consulting the district). In London, the Borough councils are the responsible authority, but the Historic Buildings and Monuments Commission have a general power of oversight over most of what they do and some concurrent powers, all of which were transferred to them when the Greater London Council was abolished. Some county councils do however have teams of specialist staff whose services are available to their constituent district authorities. The point here is that since conservation is a specialist matter it is sometimes impracticable to expect every district authority to employ a team of experts. Where they exist, such county teams have proved invaluable and of course have access to facilities such as county archives or even archaeological units which can assist with their work. In some areas where the county councils have been abolished, similar arrangements may exist by making a single district the lead authority on conservation questions, so that they can provide specialist help to the other authorities in the area.

We shall discuss planning authorities' roles with respect to listing and listed building control in the following chapters and go on
to cover their powers with regard to conservation areas, but at this
stage it would be as well to look at the machinery of control – the
administrative apparatus by which conservation is both policed and
encouraged. The key figure here, at least in most authorities, is the
conservation officer. Most planning applications are dealt with by
area teams – that is to say groups of qualified planners who have
subdivided the area of the authority between them. But in the case
of conservation, there is likely to be a designated conservation
officer who is able to offer the authority specialist advice on the
planning and often the architectural and technical aspects of individual proposals. The advent of the conservation officer has been
one of the most significant developments of the last 20 years. Before
the early 1970s there were few if any of them: now almost every
local authority has one and they are often the first and most valuable point of contact for anyone seeking consent or interested in
protecting or enhancing a particular building or area. His or her job
is to utilize the framework of controls and grants in the best way
possible. There may be a certain amount of carrot and stick in offer-
ing cocktails of grant with the threat of repairs notices being served
if a listed building is allowed to continue in a state of decay. Nor
does the conservation officer simply deal with owners. Part of
his/her job will be to keep in touch with the Commission and its
representatives both on consent applications and, where necessary,
in the construction of grant applications. Most conservation officers
have a more general remit to keep in touch with local amenity
societies (a rich source of manual labour and sometimes hard cash)
and to raise public awareness about conservation generally. A good
conservation officer can usually have more influence for good or ill
over the heritage than any other individual member of the planning
staff.

Council officers are unlikely to be able to determine anything but
the most minor consent applications. That will be the job of the
planning or development committee (the name varies) of the
Council. This will consist of councillors from most if not all the
groups represented on the Council. They will not be experts and
most will be there because they have expressed an interest in the
subject. It is one of the great strengths of the British planning
system that most decisions are taken by people who would claim no
expertise in the subject but who have nevertheless a mandate from

their voters. However expert the advice tendered by the Council officers, the final planning decision is leavened by an element of lay judgment and (we must hope!) by straightforward common sense. The councillors will have a report from the planning officers before them and this will usually, but not always, end with a recommendation on whether the consent application should be granted or refused; but there is no obligation on the councillors to accept this. They are perfectly free to substitute their own decision, and they frequently do. Their decision is likely to be final so far as the Council is concerned, although there may be an opportunity to overturn a decision of the planning committee at full Council. In effect, as soon as the planning committee have made their decision, the outcome is decided, and if the consent is granted, the developer is free to proceed with their plans. The committee are also likely to consider and decide any accompanying planning application at the same time, so that the two matters can be taken forward in tandem. The committee will in addition normally authorize the service of repairs notices and may be concerned with enforcement action against breaches of listed building control.

All this sounds very cosy and efficient. And in the majority of cases it is. But there are sources of public concern. One is about the type of situation that can arise when a Council itself has an interest in the outcome of an application. The law is clear in stating that planning authorities must make their own applications for listed building consent to the Secretary of State. But what of applications made by developers where, to put it in its broadest terms, the Council stands to benefit if consent is granted? The problem here is very similar to the one of planning gain that is found in normal development control. It is difficult for the law to define (at least in statute) where the dividing line is between the interests of the community and the interests of the individual developer. The fact that heritage buildings may be at stake, or even simply that the character and appearance of a conservation area that the Council itself has designated could be jeopardized, lends a special edge to such questions in the heritage sphere.

The other main source of public concern is the way that a few authorities treat their own listed buildings. There have in the past been some horrific cases of neglect, and it is small use an authority urging an owner to maintain his listed property when the Council itself neglects its historic buildings; or in enjoining developers to act responsibly when the Council itself is seeking to demolish or to

Traditional listed buildings: *top*: a stable and coach house in Wiltshire; and *bottom*: a Grade I rotunda by 18th century architect, James Paine.

alter beyond reason one of its own listed buildings. We have for the most part seen the back of authorities who seek to drive major road schemes through conservation areas – though a few still exist – but the day of the irresponsible authority is not wholly gone: paragraphs 3.37 and 3.38 of PPG15 underline the Government's concern that local authorities should deal with their own listed buildings in ways which will be a good example to others. A vigilant and informed public is probably the only effective way to secure a more responsible attitude by the few authorities who ignore the needs of conservation, and sometimes not even embarrassing publicity or even defeat at the polls quite does the trick.

The majority of local authorities, however, are highly responsible in their attitude towards conservation. Most recognize the need to balance the interests of the conservationist and the developer and that at best the two can both be accommodated. The pressure of public opinion over the last 25 years or so has done a lot to determine the right climate, as has the firm and gently guiding hand of the DoE. Its advice has been consistent and balanced and has shown much less change of emphasis over the last decade than has been the case with general planning. More particularly, the DoE has been prepared to back up its general policy advice with firm technical advice, a trend which has now been built upon by the Commission. In Scotland, Wales and Northern Ireland the story has been essentially the same. The results – visible in every High Street and village in the land – are for the individual to judge; but there does seem to be a consensus (which does not exist on the general planning side) that conservation policies in the United Kingdom have worked. Much of the credit for that belongs to the planning authorities, who have held the ring between the conflicting forces at work, and who have built upon their success to devise and implement schemes using both public and private sector finance and their own and voluntary efforts. Government has given them the key role in conservation. Most of them have played their part very well.

4.7
The voluntary bodies

The voluntary bodies can be divided into two categories: those whose prime aim is practical conservation work, and those whose main purpose is simply to lobby Government, either generally or on some particular aspect of conservation. Both sorts of organization harness the tremendous fund of goodwill that exists towards the conservation of the built heritage in the UK.

4.7.1 **Practical conservation work**

(a) *The National Trust*

The National Trust for Places of Historic Interest or Natural Beauty is one of the oldest and most respected conservation bodies. Founded in 1895, it embraces both the built and the natural heritage and has been an important contributor to the conservation of both. It owns over 240 historic buildings and has 2.25 million members. In 1988, more than nine million paying visitors went to its various properties making it not just the most significant mass membership organization in the conservation world but also a major force in the UK tourist industry. There is a parallel National Trust for Scotland, which was founded in 1931.

(b) *The Landmark Trust*

The Landmark Trust was founded by a former MP, John Smith, in 1965 to preserve old buildings that might not otherwise survive unspoiled. It has combined this ideal with the delightful and imaginative approach of converting them into holiday homes for letting, permitting the public to make a practical contribution towards conservation and to experience living in old buildings at first hand.

(c) *The Pilgrim Trust*

This Trust was set up by the Anglophile American Edward Hackness in 1930, and pays grants both for the preservation of individual buildings and for studies connected with conservation.

(d) *The Architectural Heritage Fund*

The AHF is one of the most valuable pieces of spin-off from European Architectural Heritage Year in 1975. It provides a cheap source of finance for local preservation trusts, supplementing capital that they raise themselves or obtain from other sources. The low interest loans enable the trusts to buy, restore and sell old buildings and to plough back proceeds into further restoration projects. The Fund sometimes enters projects on a profit-sharing basis.

The Fund is a focus for local preservation funds, convenes national conferences and issues a bulletin *Preservation in Action*. The Fund has close links with the Civic Trust and the Trust together with the DoE nominates the members of the Fund's Council of Management.

4.7.2 Lobbying work

(a) *Civic Trust*

Founded by Duncan Sandys, MP in 1957, the Trust was one of the first signs of concern at the poor quality of much modern architecture and planning. It encourages the protection and improvement of the environment, so that its concern is by no means confined to historic buildings and areas. Its Civic Trust Awards for good modern design have become an important annual event, and in addition to publishing the bi-monthly *Heritage Outlook* magazine, the Trust maintains a library and photographic collection.

The Trust was a significant force behind the *Civic Amenities Act 1967*, which led to the creation of conservation areas, and also provided the UK secretariat for European Architectural Heritage Year. It is an important source of advice to the many hundreds of local amenity societies that are registered with it. There are parallel but not totally independent Civic Trusts for the North East and the North West. There are also Civic Trusts in Scotland and Wales: that for Scotland has been given the right by the Scottish Development Department to comment on proposals to demolish or to alter radically listed buildings.

(b) *Council for British Archaeology*

The Council for British Archaeology was founded in 1944. It is the national representative body for archaeology and has extended its concern to ancient monuments and the conservation of industrial history.

(c) *Ancient Monuments Society*

In spite of its name, the Ancient Monuments Society concerns itself with protecting historic buildings of all dates. It was founded in

1924 and publishes an annual volume of transactions on architectural history.

(d) *Society for the Protection of Ancient Buildings*

The SPAB is the oldest national organization to campaign for the built heritage. It was established in 1877 by the socialist artist William Morris. In addition to its campaigning and lobbying work, the Society provides technical advice on the repair and maintenance of old buildings and organizes courses along the same lines. The Society has a particular interest in the maintenance of the original fabric of historic buildings and the avoidance of modern substitutes wherever possible.

(e) *Georgian Group*

The Group was set up in 1937 and promotes the interests of eighteenth century architecture. It lobbies in favour of the protection of Georgian buildings and has been active in saving many of them from demolition. It was founded at a time when Georgian architecture was considerably undervalued although it is as active today as ever. There is a parallel Scottish Georgian Society.

(f) *Victorian Society*

The Society aims to preserve the best of Victorian and Edwardian architecture and extends its activities into the art and history of the period. As with the SPAB and the Georgian Group, the Society was established at a time when the architecture of its period was under considerable threat and the Society has done sterling work in lobbying in favour of nineteenth and early twentieth century buildings and persuading the Secretary of State to list them when necessary. Since its foundation in 1958, the Society has taken a leading part in researching the architecture of its period, and in encouraging public interest. The Society also has regional groups which carry out casework and campaigning at the local level.

(g) *The Twentieth Century Society*

History even catches up with the amenity societies, and the Twentieth Century Society was founded as the Thirties Society in

1979 to cater for the interests of inter-war architecture. Again, growing interest in the period has helped the success of the Society and many of the best surviving buildings of the period have now been listed. Like the other amenity societies, research and a periodic newsletter are combined with frequent tours of the main buildings of the period.

(h) *The Joint Committee of the National Amenity Societies*

The Joint Committee exists as a forum co-ordinating the interests of the main national groups. Its secretariat is provided by the Ancient Monuments Society and it lobbies Government on behalf of the conservation bodies.

(i) *SAVE Britain's Heritage*

SAVE was founded by a group of journalists, architects and planners in the wake of the exhibition on *The Destruction of the English Country House* that was held at the V & A in 1974. The group has consistently produced the most polished and professional campaigns in the heritage world, using its supporters' skills to the full. SAVE is not a mass-membership organization, and does not aim to be, but it has produced a number of well-illustrated books and pamphlets highlighting threats to the heritage in the United Kingdom. This has been accompanied by some highly effective lobbying of both central and local government.

(j) *Garden History Society*

The Society is concerned with the preservation of historic gardens and landscape parks, and researches and campaigns on behalf of all aspects of garden history. This is a complementary role to those groups lobbying on behalf of the built heritage, and there is some linkage particularly in the preservation of garden structures that are listed, and in the relationship between historic houses and their grounds. Circular 9/95 states that the Society should be consulted on planning applications affecting historic parks and gardens.

This is necessarily a brief résumé of the very considerable voluntary sector. It leaves out many of the smaller national amenity bodies, the specialist groups and some societies whose interest in the built

heritage is slightly peripheral to their other activities. Most particularly, it leaves out the vast and growing number of local amenity
societies who are so effective in their own areas. There are no accu-
rate figures for the numbers of these, but one estimate is that there
are some 1200 such societies with 300000 members. That figure
alone bears witness to the public interest in conservation and, taken
together with the membership of such organizations as English
Heritage and the National Trust (although there will of course be
double and even triple counting), suggests that up to two million
people are concerned enough about the built heritage to belong to a
national or local organization. It is they who have helped place conservation squarely centre stage in any discussion about planning.

Chapter 5

LISTED BUILDINGS

5.1
What can be listed?

The basis for the listing system is section 1(1) of the Planning
(Listed Buildings & Conservation Areas) Act 1990. This simply
states that

> For the purposes of this Act and with a view to the guidance of local plan-
> ning authorities in the performance of their functions under this Act and
> the principal Act in relation to buildings of special architectural or historic
> interest, the Secretary of State shall compile lists of such buildings, or
> approve, with or without modifications, such lists compiled by the Historic
> Buildings and Monuments Commission for England ... or by other persons
> or bodies of persons, and may amend any list so compiled or approved ...

From this, it is easy enough to infer what a list is: but how to define
a building?

The only guidance here is in the Town & Country Planning Act
1990, which gives what can only be described as a partial definition.
It states that

> 'building' includes any structure or erection, and any part of a building, as
> so defined, but does not include plant or machinery comprised in a build-
> ing;

So we know that the definition includes 'any structure or erection'
(but of course the wording of the Act can be construed to imply that
other things might be included as well); and we know that plant or
machinery are excluded (but no doubt are many other things). How
far does the legal definition actually get us?

In short, it does not help us much at all, and since the question of a definition has not been directly tested in the Courts in recent times, there is no useful precedent to go on either. In the circumstances, the most reliable guide is the advice set out in PPG15 (paragraphs 3.30–3.32) and a look at what the Secretary of State actually does list – though we must state again that unless and until the Departmental policy is tested in the Courts, or clarified by revising legislation, it cannot be considered to be definitive. With this caveat, we can say that the Department relies in practice on the 'structure or erection' element of the definition in section 336. The Act does not help us further, since it does not give a definition of structure and provides a definition of erection which is not really useful for our purposes. Instead, there seem to be two tests.

1. Is the object (for want of a better word) three-dimensional? Most 'buildings' in lay terms would pass this test, as would most structures and anything that was erected.
2. In the case of fixtures, is the object securely fixed either by dint of its foundation or some other method?

Again, it is worth emphasizing that these tests have no legal basis, but are based on an interpretation of the law. In practice, they mean that there is a wide variety of objects that are eligible for listing, and these are reflected in the lists. In addition to conventional buildings (again to use the lay term), tombstones, pillar boxes, bollards, pumps, stocks, telephone kiosks, gate posts and even docks have been included. All satisfy the two tests set out above. On the other hand, pathways have been excluded from the lists, since, although they have a foundation, they do not, except on the most narrow of definitions, have three dimensions (but an artificially raised pathway – a causeway for instance – may be listed because it is a structure in the view of the Department).

Most of the problematical cases have revolved around objects that while satisfying test 1, enter muddy waters on test 2. Architectural features like chimney breasts or panelling clearly fail on test 2, but what of the statues and decorative urns that are found in the grounds of some of our country houses. Some of these may be fixed in the earth, by some sort of foundation, and these easily pass test 2. Others, however, may simply rest on stone plinths, and are effectively secured to the ground by their own weight. Since these may vary from quite large objects to those that could be picked up and carried away, a further test is applied to assess whether they are eligible for listing. This is

2. (a) If the object were to be removed, does it need to be demolished or taken down; or can it be simply taken away as it is?

Even this leaves a grey area: some objects can be taken away by a large crane, although it might be as easy to dismantle them and take them away in parts. In cases where the Secretary of State and an owner disagreed on such an object's eligibility for listing, then it would be for the Courts to decide between the two parties. The only legal guidance here (on which the Department's procedures is based) is Lord Scarman's judgment in the case of *Berkley* v. *Poulett*:

an object, resting on the ground by its own weight alone, can be a fixture, if it be so heavy that there is no need to tie it into a foundation and if it were put in place to improve the realty. Prima facie, however, an object resting on the ground by its own weight alone is not a fixture.

As a footnote to this section, it is worth pointing out that natural features that have been adapted to fulfil the function of buildings are not normally listed. An example would be houses constructed in the side of rock faces either by hollowing out or by using caves (such places do exist!). Presumably in such cases it could be argued that no human made foundation exists: certainly the insertion of floors and windows would give such places a three-dimensional existence.

5.2
The criteria for listing

There are two sets of criteria for listing: the statutory criteria contained in the 1990 Act, and the non-statutory criteria prescribed by the Secretary of State on the recommendation of his expert advisers.

Section 1(1) sets out one overall test for assessing a building's listability: does it possess special architectural or historic interest? It nowhere defines this all-important term, so the Secretary of State is given the maximum discretion in judging exactly what is special architectural or historic interest. His decision is final, although it could be tested in the Courts through judicial review if it was felt that he had acted unreasonably. Section 1(4) of the Act requires the Secretary of State to consult with the Historic Buildings and

Monuments Commission and with 'such other persons or bodies of persons as appear to him appropriate as having special knowledge of, or interest in, buildings of architectural or historic interest' but it does not oblige him to heed what they say.

In applying the test of special interest, the Act points to two specific features of the building that the Secretary of State may (but not must) take into account. These are set out in section 1(3) and comprise:

(a) any respect in which the exterior of the building contributes to the architectural or historic interest of any group of which it forms part: this is the so-called group value of the building;
(b) the architectural or historic interest of any feature of the building consisting of a man-made object or structure fixed to the building or located within its curtilage.

The definition in section 1(3)(b) is slightly curious, since it could be interpreted as including all that plant and machinery that is excluded from the definition of 'building'. Presumably it can be inferred from this that although it would not be possible to list a freestanding piece of machinery (since this is excluded from the definition of building) it would be possible to list a historically uninteresting building, if it had fixed within it or to it a piece of machinery (such as a waterwheel or mill machinery) which possessed a sufficient degree of architectural or historic interest. The non-statutory criteria for listing are those by which the Secretary of State defines special architectural or historic interest. Those currently in force were originally promulgated in March 1970 on the recommendation of the then Historic Buildings Council, and as we saw in the last chapter they have been modified subsequently not least to take account of the listing of inter-war and most recently modern buildings. They are set out in Appendix A.

Particular difficulties arise with the application of the criteria to derelict or partially derelict buildings. It is sometimes a source of annoyance or even amusement to owners to find dilapidated structures listed on account of their special interest. There are no hard and fast rules here. A building may still fall within the definition of a structure or erection even when half of it has fallen down. It may still possess special interest even if it is not complete: after all, we become very excited about finding a Roman villa, even though we are lucky if more than the foundations are still evident. In the same way, some buildings may have special interest even though they are only partially complete – particularly if they are of an early or rare building type. There may be a point where a building is so derelict that it no longer has any special interest. But the fact that a structure is dilapidated does not of itself make it unlistable.

The same goes for buildings that have been altered or extended or partially demolished. The degree of alteration or demolition will certainly be taken into account in deciding whether to list, and the rarity of the original structure will again be a relevant factor, but fcw buildings survive completely unaltered for long, and the inspectors will not in most instances be looking just for buildings in pristine condition.

5.3
Grading

Listed buildings are divided into three grades. There is no provision for these in the statutes, but the grades have acquired a particular importance both for grant purposes, and more particularly for listed building consent procedure. Since the directions given about procedure in consent cases relate to their grading, the system has in fact been given a kind of quasi-legal status.

The three grades which buildings are given in the lists are as follows:

Grade I: these are buildings of outstanding or exceptional interest, such as the great cathedrals and stately homes and very good examples of building types which are uncommon; in all some 9000 buildings (about 2% of the total) are included on the list at Grade I.
Grade II*: these are particularly important buildings of more than special interest but not in the outstanding class; some of the second division country houses and churches are in this category – an estimated 4% of the total numbers of listed buildings.
Grade II: these comprise the remainder of our listed buildings – about 94% of the total, buildings which are of special interest but which are not sufficiently important to be counted among the élite.

As we noted in the last chapter, there used to be a non-statutory Grade III, which was found on the lists drawn up as part of the first survey. This grading has now been phased out, although it may be found still in the old lists where they survive, and seems to enjoy a particular longevity in estate agents' particulars where it is virtually meaningless. It was used to signify buidings of local interest, and in fact most of these have been upgraded to II in the course of the resurvey.

Up to 1977, Anglican churches in use enjoyed a different form of grading. They were categorized as Grade A, B or C. These were not exactly analogous to I, II* and II, although they did denote the degree of special interest in the church building. Many resurvey lists – those produced up to 1977 – had the alphabetical grading for churches; some of these have been amended to Roman numeral grading where their quality has been reassessed by the Secretary of State in considering a grant application for them.

5.4
How buildings are listed

5.4.1 General procedure

The end of the national resurvey means that the listing programme is substantially complete. But some additions to the list are still being made. These comprise

1. Buildings which are in areas covered at the start of the resurvey where the list is now considered defective.
2. As a variant of this, buildings in areas covered by later lists which are now regarded as listable. This may simply reflect fresh knowledge or developments in public taste which have altered the perception of special interest.This is particularly true of late Victorian and twentieth century buildings, where the criteria have been interpreted more liberally with the passage of time. In other areas, such as the English Arts and Crafts style and vernacular architecture, scholarship has developed over the last 25 years and some buildings have consequently crossed the threshold of listability.
3. Building types which are underrepresented in the lists, which English Heritage are now tackling on a thematic basis.
4. Buildings which have simply been overlooked. They may simply have failed to catch the fieldworker's eye, possibly because they were in an area of undistinguished buildings; or some fresh evidence of their special interest has come to light.

Few buildings are listed without a site inspection from one of English Heritage's inspectors. They are bound by a Code of

Conduct, and copies of this are available from the Department of National Heritage. Briefly, they are instructed not to trespass on land, to make efforts to contact owners and occupiers of the buildings they visit and to co-operate with owners as far as possible.

It has often been asked why inspectors do not make appointments to carry out their inspections. There are two reasons for this. First, a few unscrupulous owners, if forewarned that an inspector was coming, might take steps to mutilate or destroy buildings which they did not want to be listed. This can particularly apply to derelict or empty buildings. Secondly, the administrative effort required would be considerable. Inspectors need to inspect many buildings which turn out on a close look to be below the line for listing. To notify everyone of a visit – and this without any ability to state with accuracy a date or time – would be impractical. But the end of the resurvey now means that the numbers of buildings being listed annually will drop. The Government are accordingly now looking again at whether a further degree of consultation would be possible, and in March 1995, as a first step, announced that they were consulting the public on English Heritage's latest list of recommendations affecting modern buildings.

Inspectors normally begin by looking at the exterior of the building. This will usually give an idea of its date, form or function. They will then photograph the building – an essential element in the Secretary of State's decision whether to list – and probably seek an internal inspection. If the owner is out, the inspector will leave his/her card and seek to make contact later. In a few cases, an internal inspection may not be possible, either because the owner or occupier cannot be traced or because he or she refuses admittance. In these cases, the inspector simply has to make the best assessment possible on the basis of the evidence available. It would be possible to call on the powers of access available under the law to enforce entry: but this would scarcely be a good advertisement for conservation, and, as we remarked in Chapter 3, it was not found necessary in the entire course of the resurvey in England to use this power. Owners have almost universally been highly co-operative with inspectors; pride of ownership and a natural desire to learn more of the history of their properties are the motivating factors.

The internal inspection is usually very important in the assessment. It often adds to the understanding of the property, not least because internal features have survived where external detail of interest may have been obscured by later alterations. East Anglia

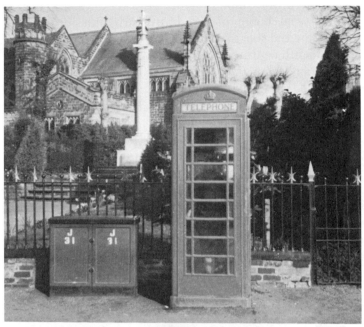

The diversity of the lists: *top*: Scott's classic design of the K6 telephone kiosk; *bottom*: an Edwardian theatre in London.

has some startling examples of this kind. The town houses put up during the wool boom of the fourteenth and fifteen centuries decayed during the subsequent 300 years. When prosperity returned in the eighteenth century, the houses were given a new plaster coating which concealed their medieval origins. Quite simply, they were gentrified. In cases like these – and local examples are found all over the country – internal inspection is essential. Devon is particularly rich in this type of building, while one of the most spectacular examples was a row of perfectly ordinary looking houses in an Essex village: they seemed like a twentieth century terrace, with their modern windows and doors but there was something odd about the pitch of the roof. Inside was a fourteenth century hall house, to all intents and purposes invisible from the road. The first survey of historic buildings in England ignored almost entirely the interiors of buildings, and it is not surprising that the resurvey lists grew as the inspectors carried out their detective work, looking for telltale signs that a building may be a lot older than it appears.

B   Building-type – the original purpose for which the building was constructed. followed by the present use, if different.

D   Date – the date of construction of the building and any additions or alterations made subsequently.

A   Architect – if any.

M   Materials – in the order structure, cladding, decoration, roof.

P   Plan/style – a general description of its style and layout.

F   Facades – a detailed description of the exterior of the building.

I   Interior – a description of any significant interior features.

S   Subsidiary features – such as garden railings, small extensions.

H   History – the history of the building (if of interest), or its association with well known characters or events.

E   Extra information – perhaps its setting, its connection with a famous collection of art or furniture.

S   Sources – any relevant sources of information from which the description has been compiled.

Figure 5.1 The form of the list description.

The inspector's draft lists are submitted with his or her photographs to the supervising inspector. Each entry has a serial number and a grid reference, as well as an address and a proposed grading and a note of any group value. The list description sets out the most important features of the building. Simply because a feature is not present, some think it is not covered by the listing; this is not so. Listing covers the entire building, but the description focuses only on those elements which are of particular interest (of course, the whole building is of special interest, but in some cases this may be by virtue of special features: we discussed this point in section 5.2). In some instances the list description may say what is not of special interest – a twentieth century extension for example – although even these features are covered by the listing. The list description is set out in a prescribed form, known by the utterly unmemorable mnemonic B DAMP FISHES (Figure 5.1). There is no prescribed length for a list description: the shortest are one-liners, the longest is seven pages; nor does the length of the description necessarily reflect the importance of the building – Chiswick House, the masterpiece of English Palladianism, has a list description only four lines long.

5.4.2 Spot-listing requests

In addition to the investigative work of English Heritage it is open to anyone to bring a candidate for spot-listing to the attention of the Secretary of State. Paragraph 6.21 of PPG15 asks that such requests should be made, if possible, well in advance of development proposals being realized, so that developers do not find their plans stymied at the last moment by spot-listing. In practice, a large proportion of spot-listing requests come from local authorities themselves, and are made at an early stage so that if necessary any application for listed building consent can be considered in tandem with the planning application for the new development.

Requests to spot-list should be sent to the Department of National Heritage (and not the Commission) and to its equivalent bodies in Scotland, Wales and Northern Ireland. They should be accompanied by an address or a location plan together with up-to-date photographs of the building and any information that may be available about its age and history. Once the Department receive the request to spot-list, they will assess the degree of urgency attached to the case (usually with the help of the local authority) and send the request to the Commission with a deadline. In some cases, the request can be turned down without reference to the Commission – for instance, where the area has been recently resurveyed and there is no evidence to suggest the building was overlooked, or where it clearly fails to meet the criteria.

From the Commission's point of view, spot-listing is a very costly and inefficient process. The photographs allow one of their inspectors to establish if there is a prima facie case for a site visit, and if it is concluded that there is, it generally means that a special journey is necessary to look at the building. This has to be done within the Department's deadline and sometimes has to be fitted in with other work. The recommendation must then be forwarded quickly to the Department for decision. The surprising thing is that the system, which operates as a permanent type of crisis management, works very well. Few buildings are lost and in general developers co-operate (though understandably not always willingly) to allow assessments to be made. Spot-listing can and has been carried out in under 24 hours from the time of the receipt of the request. No-one particularly likes the system but, in an imperfect world, it is difficult to envisage an alternative.

5.5

Building preservation notices

Local planning authorities have their own power to extend temporary control over a building which they consider to be of special architectural or historic interest. Under section 3 of the 1990 Act, a planning authority may serve a building preservation notice, which has the effect of extending listed building control to the building for a period of up to six months. During this time, the Secretary of State for National Heritage will consider whether he should add the building to the list. If he does, the notice is confirmed and the building is immediately listed. If he decides not to, the notice lapses immediately and with it the listed building control. Occasionally, the six month period ends without the Secretary of State having confirmed or rejected the notice. This is sometimes because authorities are slow in sending notices to the Department: it is not unknown for authorities to delay sending the notice until three of its six months' currency has lapsed, which can cause problems in arranging a speedy assessment. It has been known for authorities to

The mainstay of the lists: *top*: the country house (Nunwell, Brading, Isle of Wight); and *bottom*: the local church (St Mary's, Merton Park, London)

serve a second notice on occasion, but such instances are rare, and where the lapsing of the first notice has occurred because the Secretary of State has decided not to list the property, the authority is leaving itself open to the charge that it has acted unreasonably unless it has very good reason for its action – for example fresh information.

Not surprisingly, the Department prefers an authority to serve a Building Preservation Notice than to seek a spot-listing. Paragraph 6.23 of PPG15 enjoins authorities to take this course, although few of them do so. The reasons are twofold. First, the notice is a legal document and will require the authority's legal officers to draw it up. This takes time, and they may be reluctant to draw up a document with which they are not familiar. Secondly, and probably more saliently, there is a sting in the tail. If a notice is not confirmed by the Secretary of State, an owner can seek compensation from the local authority in respect of any loss that has occurred as a result of their action. If contractors have had to stand down as a result of the notice, for instance, any penalty fee could be payable by the local authority. The provision was included to concentrate the minds of local planners and ensure that notices were not served without justification. Unfortunately, perhaps as a result, most authorities prefer to request spot-lists – often at short notice and posing considerable logistical problems for both the Commissioin and the Department. Building Preservation Notices are a much more effective and efficient tool which should, ideally, avoid the need for last-minute spot-listing in all but a handful of cases.

5.6
The Secretary of State's decision

Once the Secretary of State has received a recommendation for listing from the Commission, his role is very much that of an editor in a publishing-house. The lists have to be checked to see that they conform to the prescribed format. Spelling is checked and, where possible, the draft is sent to the local authority so that it can check the accuracy of addresses and suggest any additions or alterations to what the Commission has proposed.

The lists then go forward for signature. Nominally, the decision is the Secretary of State's but, in all but a few cases, the decision will be taken by the Head of the Department's Listing Branch, who is of middle management grade. He/she will however refer controversial recommendations to the junior Minister responsible for heritage matters, and a few cases will reach the Secretary of State himself.

In 99% of cases, the Secretary of State will accept the advice of the Commission about a building's listability, but the decision is ultimately his. He is not bound to accept the Commision's advice, and in a number of cases he declines to do so. This ensures that an important leavening of lay judgment is added to the views of the experts. Listing can only succeed if it maintains public confidence and if it continues to reflect public taste. While expert advice is welcome in establishing facts about the case, that advice must be seen in a broader context of national policy and public opinion. Experts, after all, have their fashions and whims, and they are not always those of the public at large. There is a second reason for ensuring that the decision on listing is left with the Secretary of State: he is answerable to Parliament for what he does, so that listing is open to the normal democratic processes in this country. English Heritage is a quango and it is not directly answerable to Parliament.

The Secretary of State's right to reject English Heritage's recommendation was tested in the Courts by the Victorian Society, who sought judicial review of his refusal to list St Mark's Church in Horsham. The application was rejected. The judge upheld the Secretary of State's decision. Section 1(4) of the 1990 Act is abundantly clear: the Secretary of State is only obliged to consult the Commission, not to heed what they say. It is an interesting legal point to ponder whether the Court's decision would have been the same if a chorus of voices and expert bodies had raised a demand for listing. Would the Secretary of State then have been acting unreasonably to fly in the face of them all? The wording of the Act certainly suggests that the outcome would have been the same.

However, one thing is certain: once the Secretary of State is satisfied that a building has special architectural or historic interest, he is bound by duty to list it. That is the import of section 1(1) of the 1990 Act. It does not matter how inconvenient or politically awkward his decision may be, the duty is absolute. This is one of the few areas of listing that has reached in the Courts in the so-called Johnny Walker case we mentioned in section 3.5. This arose in 1977 when the late listing of a London warehouse caused its redevelopment value to drop dramatically. The Courts upheld the

Secretary of State's decision; he had accepted the recommendation of his statutory advisers and so had no option but to list. That remains the position today. The Secretary of State is unable in taking his decision to make any allowance for other factors, such as the merits of any redevelopment plans (even presumably, if he has granted permission for these himself). His reasons for including or excluding a building from the lists must relate solely to special architectural or historic factors.

5.7
Action after the list is signed

The list takes effect immediately it is signed. The local authority are notified as soon as this occurs. Moreover, since breaches of listed building control are offences of strict liability – in other words, ignorance is no defence – the Department writes to the owner or occupier of the building by first class post on the same day, warning them that they will require listed building consent for any work affecting the building. In recent years, the previously rather stiff letter has been revised to be more user-friendly, and an explanatory guide on the effect of listing is also enclosed.

Inevitably, a certain number of letters do not reach their addresses, and where the threat to the building may be more urgent, the Department's letter is usually sent by recorded delivery. This at least ensures that there is a record of whether the letter has been received, which may be useful if a breach subsequently occurs.

The Department's letter is only an early warning. Under section 2(3), local planning authorities (in this case, the district or borough council) are obliged to serve a statutory notice on the owner and occupier of the building informing them of the listing. Since authorities know that the Department's warning letter has already gone out, they may be some time in doing this: delays of one to two years were not unknown in the case of whole resurvey lists. The point here is that only the local authority will have access to the names and addresses of every owner and occupier. The Department's letters can only be addressed impersonally, and in the case of unoccupied buildings it may not be possible to send a letter at all unless the Department has some special knowledge of who they are. (There is one possibly apocryphal story of a letter being addressed to 'The Occupier, Milestone on the A31 ...'). The local authority must also register the listing as a land charge, so that it will turn up in solicitors' searches in due course.

The list is now public property. It can be inspected at the offices of county, regional or district councils or at the National Monuments Record, which forms part of the Royal Commission on Historical Monuments (they are also now the repository for all the photographs that accompany the Commission's recommendations to list). Copies are not on sale to the public for the good reason that demand would be insufficient to warrant a long print run, so that the price of any published list would be prohibitive.

However, English Heritage and the RCHM will have placed the lists on computer by April 1996 and this should greatly improve their availability.

5.8
Appeals against listing

There is no statutory right of appeal against listing. This is because decisions to list are taken against a set of objective criteria, so that appeals should not be necessary. In any case, there is little demand for a right of appeal. As we noted in Chapter 3, when defending the existing system in the House of Lords in 1986, the then Minister, Lord Skelmersdale, said that out of 23 000 buildings listed in the preceding year only some three dozen had been the subject of representations from their owners; and of these only five had been found to be justified. To construct a full-blown appeals mechanism, with all the paraphernalia of inspectors and inquiries, would be redundant. Instead, there are two mechanisms for appealing against the listing decision.

First, it is possible to cite, as grounds in any appeal against the refusal of listed building consent, the fact that a building should not have been included in the list in the first place. Provision for this is included in section 21(3) of the 1990 Act, and only one or two cases a year take advantage of it. The point here is that listing should not affect owners except in so far as they need listed building consent to carry out any works of alterations, extension or demolition. Thus there is a logic in allowing owners to appeal against the listing itself if their application for consent is refused. At that point, of course, the machinery of an appeal against the consent is set in motion anyway, so that the testing of the building's special interest involves no extra effort on anyone's part.

The second mechanism is the so-called informal appeals mechanism. Strictly speaking, appeal is the wrong word here: it is a right of representation, and it is essentially only the 'right' which any citizen has to make representations against a decision which appears to him/her to be unreasonable. The procedure has been used primarily to correct errors on the list. These do occur from time to time. Neo-Georgian houses of *circa* 1970 have been mistaken on occasion for the real thing, and the author has to admit responsibility for accepting English Heritage's advice to list what seemed a sixteenth century house at Sea Palling in Norfolk which proved subsequently to have been lovingly assembled from weathered brick and old timbers and even to have been given a convincing slope in the floorboards of the upper storey!

Any owner or occupier who feels that a building does not possess the special interest claimed for it may write to the Department. There are no forms to fill in and no procedural hoops to go through. All that is required is a map or an address, some photographs and any information that is available that shows the listing decision to have been wrong. The Commission will notify the local authorities concerned and the national amenity societies (see section 6.2) of the request to delist. They will then despatch a different inspector from the one who made the original recommendation to look at the property and to make a further recommendation. That advice will again go to the Department and a decision will be taken as if the case is a new one. The informality of this system probably ensures that more people use the system than would do so if statutory mechanisms were involved. But the important point is the one contained in the last section. The Secretary of State can only consider the special architectural or historic merits of the building. No other factors are relevant, and so appeals should be framed with this in mind. The Department produces a very helpful leaflet on appeals which is available from them free of charge.

5.9
Certificates of immunity from listing

As we have seen, the late listing of buildings can cause problems for developers (and indeed ordinary householders) if their plans are thrown into disarray, or even if they are simply delayed. Concern about this led in 1980 to a new procedure now set out in section 6 of the Act. This provides that where a planning permission is being sought or has been granted, anybody may apply to the Secretary of State for a certificate of immunity from listing in respect of the building in question. The effect of the certificate is to prevent the Secretary of State from listing the building, and the planning authority from serving a building preservation notice, for a period of five years (i.e. the usual currency of a planning permission).

The certificate procedure thus gives developers the certainty they seek about listing before they invest time and money in their plans, but it is of course a double-edged sword. If in the course of his consideration, the Secretary of State decides the building does have special interest, his statutory duty under section 1(1) compels him to list it; so an application is a gamble. But if used wisely by the developer, i.e. at the very outset of working up plans (perhaps in tandem with an outline planning application), the certificate can be a useful form of defence.

Applications for certificates of immunity are sent to the Department. There is no application form and no fee. Notice of the application has to be given to the local planning authority (and in London also to English Heritage), and the Department will normally consider any representations they make alongside the advice of the Commission. A plan showing the position of the building, together with photographs of the exterior and interior and any known information about its history or construction should be supplied with the application.

The Department will always ask the Commission to carry out a very thorough cellar to attic inspection of the building. Because of this, PPG15 warns that any earlier decision on listability is set aside by the application for a certificate, because the building is reassessed so thoroughly (since this is effectively the last chance there will be to list the building in its present form). A recommendation will go to the Secretary of State in the normal way, and a decision taken. This will be notified both to the applicant and to the local planning authority.

One curiosity of the system is that the CoI does not grant immunity from the need to seek conservation area consent if demolition is involved (see Chapter 7). This is because the factors to be taken into account in the latter case are slightly different – namely the contribution of the building to the character and appearance of the conservation area rather than its intrinsic special interest.

5.10
Delisting

Buildings can be taken off as well as added to the lists. This occurs in three situations.

1. Where an appeal against a listing decision is successful. Since there is no time-limit on the right to make representations, an appeal can be made at any time (perhaps when a new owner feels the listing was unjustified).
2. Where a building is no longer considered to be of special interest. At the end of every draft resurvey list, there is a sad little section of buildings which were considered listable at the first survey, but which are no longer considered to be of special interest because of the alterations and modifications carried out to them – usually with the necessary listed building consent. The delisting of such buildings often causes much more distress to owners than the addition of properties to the list: many see it (not without reason) as a commentary on their stewardship of the property.
3. Where a building has been demolished, with or without consent, it is often removed from the list. We have to say 'often' because the deletion is not automatic unless and until the Department are notified that the building has disappeared. Buildings which have been drastically altered may also be delisted.

As with listing, the Secretary of State is obliged to consult the Commission before removing a building from the list. This is done by a simple delisting document similar to that used for spot-listing or amendments. Again as with listing, local authorities are obliged under the Act to notify owners and occupiers of the Secretary of State's decision.

5.11
Conclusion

Given the size and scope of the exercise, the listing of buildings in Britain has been something of an organizational triumph. At the height of the resurvey exercise, the Department of the Environment was issuing 36 new resurvey lists a month and spot-listing over 1000 buildings a year. All this was achieved with a workforce in the Department, English Heritage and the private and public sector fieldwork agents that barely topped 100. The machinery for listing works well and profits from the cooperation of local authorities and owners of listed and listable buildings. As a result, Britain has registers of its architectural heritage which are unique in the Western World. The effort came too late to save the gems we lost in the 50 years up to 1970. But it came soon enough to save many more that would otherwise have been preserved only in photographs by now.

Chapter 6

LISTED BUILDING CONTROL

6.1
Introduction

The statutory lists are only a register. Their purpose is to identify those buildings which are of special interest, so that the case for their conservation can be looked at separately from the merits of any planning application that affects them. Two points spring from this which are worth underlining.

In the first place, unless a building is listed or situated in a conservation area, there is no form of control which permits its special interest to be considered in this way. Listed building control allows a pause for reflection and a chance for vetoing or modifying any proposals to alter or demolish the building. It is in fact quite possible for planning permission to be granted but for listed building consent to be refused: and without both, the development cannot proceed.

The second point is one we touched upon in the opening chapter. The emphasis is on conservation rather than preservation. In many cases, the two will be synonymous, but in others, the emphasis will not be on keeping the building as it is at all costs, but in ensuring that its life is guaranteed and lengthened in a way that will not destroy its special interest. That means in many cases that there will be a balance to be struck between the value of the old and the needs of the new. In others, no balance will be possible and consent will have to be refused. In every case, it is the purpose of listed building control to make this kind of judgment.

The guiding provision for listed building control is section 7 of the 1990 Act. This states that

... no person shall execute or cause to be executed any works for the demolition of a listed building or for its alteration or extension in any manner
which would affect its character as a building of special architectural or
historic interest, unless the works are authorized.

The definition of listed building here is that given in section 1(5)
and is a lot clearer than our attempts in the last chapter to define
buildings that could be listed. Simply, a listed building is any
building which is included for the time being in the lists, and any
object or structure within the curtilage of the building which was
erected prior to 1 July 1948. This last proviso removes the anom-
alous position which existed up to 1986 when any modern shed or
garage required listed building consent for its removal despite the
fact that it might have been *in situ* for 20 years or less.

6.2
Planning and listed building control

Listed building control is part of the planning system. It sits alongside
normal development control, which operates in general through a
system of planning permissions, and it has a parallel regime for
appeals and enforcement. But the law for the most part clearly
separates out the case for conserving a building from the case for the
development proposals affecting it. So where such proposals come
forward, separate planning and listed building consent applications
must be made to the planning authority. In general, they will be
considered together; but officers and councillors will be aware that
different factors are relevant to each application.

There has been some attempt to link the two sorts of control.
Firstly, section 66 of the 1990 Act requires that planning applications involving listed buildings or their settings should take account
of their special interest and, in the latter case, under section 67,
should be advertised locally. This restates a provision originally
included in the 1971 Act. A separate direction sets out the categories of applications affecting the setting of listed buildings or the
character and appearance of conservation areas which must be notified to English Heritage.

Secondly, the Town & Country Planning Act 1990 has given a
new importance to development plans. Section 54A states that any
planning decision must be made in accordance with the development plan unless material considerations indicate otherwise.

Paragraph 2.3 of PPG15 states that plans should set out clearly all conservation policies that are relevant to planning authorities' development control functions, including areas where development and conservation issues are to be addressed together.

This is a slightly awkward area, for the Courts have clarified the fact that section 54A cannot apply to listed building or conservation area consent because there is no statutory requirement in these cases to have regard to the development plan. So section 54A can only apply to the planning application. This means that criteria relevant to listed building consent applications but which are not subject to planning permission – such as interior alterations – cannot be included in the development plan, the circular suggesting that these might be the subject instead of supplementary planning guidance.

The criteria to be included in development plans are necessarily broad brush. PPG15 states that the strategic structure plan (or first part of a unitary development plan) might include guidance on the approach local plans should adopt on such issues as the capacity of historic towns to sustain development, the relief that might be obtained for historic central areas by identifying growth opportunities elsewhere or the provision of a transport infrastructure which respects the historic environment. Local plans (or the second part of UDPs) should set out more detailed guidance concerning, for instance, particular areas or building types, or new development affecting the setting of listed buildings. But the PPG warns that guidance should not be over-prescriptive nor too inflexible in relation to individual buildings and groups of buildings.

PPG15 itself sets out national guidance on development control issues touching on conservation. It covers:

1. the need for early consultation with planning authorities on development proposals affecting historic buildings or areas (paragraph 2.11);
2. the design of new buildings, which needs careful consideration where they sit alongside historic buildings: in such cases, scale, height, massing and the use of suitable materials will be important (paragraph 2.14);
3. the setting of listed buildings (paragraphs 2.16–2.17);
4. changes of use, where the advice is to exercise sympathetic controls where this would give an historic building a new lease of life (paragraph 2.18).

Much of this reiterates earlier advice given in Circular 8/87. But

PPG15 does also include new sections on World Heritage Sites, historic battlefields and the wider historic landscape. While these are not necessarily covered by listing, the principle of such registers is extended to them in the form of an acknowledgement of their importance in framing planning policies and exercising development control.

6.3

Procedure for obtaining listed building consent

Applications for listed building consent must be made to local planning authorities, although as we shall see the decision is sometimes taken by the Secretary of State. The requirement and procedure for obtaining consent is prescribed in sections 7–26 of the 1990 Act and in regulations made under it. These are summarized in Figures 6.1 and 6.2. Copies of application forms are available from planning authorities. Briefly, the application should:

- identify the building, including by relation to a plan;
- set out the work proposed, and should be accompanied by plans and drawings showing what this comprises;
- include any other particulars required by the authority.

In addition, in the case of an application to demolish all or part of a listed building, it is helpful to include photographs of all the parts that are to be demolished, or of all the elevations and features of special interest in the case of total demolition. No fee is payable when an application is made. Applicants for consent must also provide a certificate (the form of which is prescribed in the regulations) showing either that they:

- own the property concerned; or
- have notified the owner of the application (owner is defined as the freeholder or a leaseholder with not less than seven years of the lease outstanding).

This provision is similar to that for applicants for planning permission.

Once the application has been received, the planning authority is required to advertise it in a local newspaper and either on or near to the site to which the application relates. The regulations also state

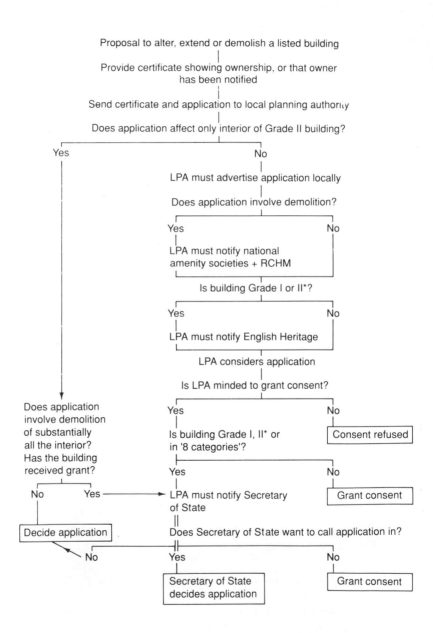

Figure 6.1 Listed building consent – all areas except London.

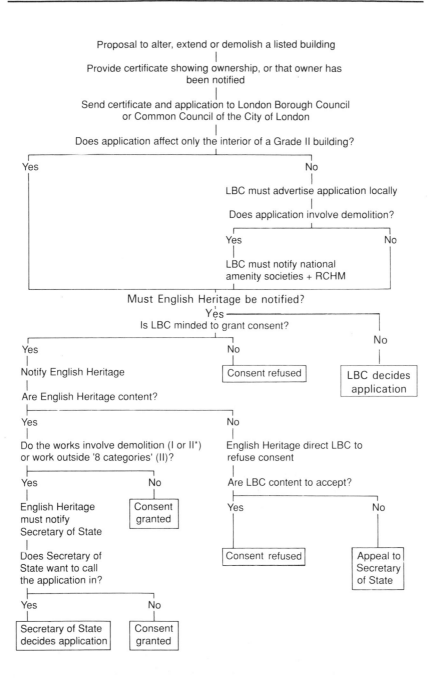

Figure 6.2 Listed building consent – London only.

specifically that the authority should take account of any representations they receive. However, the requirement to advertise does
not apply to applications which relate only to the interior of Grade
II buildings.

Since the lists are national in their scope, it is only fair that
notification of proposals affecting a listed building should go to
national as well as local bodies. Under sections 15(5) and (6) of the
1990 Act, the Secretary of State has a power to direct local planning
authorities to notify specified persons of applications for consent
and of the decisions taken on them. This allows national bodies to
have their say and saves them relying on local members or a comprehensive scanning of local papers to keep up to date with the
applications that are in the pipeline. The Secretary of State has
accordingly directed that notification of all applications for consent
to demolish a listed building, and of the ensuing decisions, should
be given to

The Ancient Monuments Society
The Council for British Archaeology
The Society for the Protection of Ancient Buildings
The Georgian Group
The Victorian Society
The Royal Commission on the Historical Monuments of England.

It is a pity that there is so much needless duplication here. It is
unlikely for instance that the Victorian Society will want to comment on an application concerning a medieval building, or that the
Georgians will become exercised about a mid-nineteenth century
structure: it would clearly be simpler if authorities were directed to
send copies of applications and decisions to one central clearing
house servicing all the societies which could then decide who would
be interested in what. It is doubly a pity since the framework for
such a clearing house exists in both the Joint Committee of the
National Amenity Societies and the Commission, but the situation
persists, and for the present local planning authorities are stuck with
it. As a footnote, it should be said that the position of the Royal
Commission is rather different, not least because it is not a voluntary body and because its role is not a lobbying one so much as that
of an archive, as we shall see shortly. In their case, the purpose of
notification is to enable them to supply factual material about the
building (if available) from their records and to be prepared to record
it in the event that consent for demolition is granted.

The Secretary of State has made a separate direction in the case of English Heritage. It has been directed that English Heritage should be notified of all applications for consent to

- alter, extend, or demolish any Grade I or II* building *outside* Greater London; and to
- alter, extend or demolish any grade of listed building *inside* Greater London.

In addition, it is now proposed that notification of English Heritage should also apply to applications affecting Grade II buildings outside London, when a significant degree of demolition is involved.

Again, authorities are required to notify the Commission of the decisions they take in these cases. If the Commission does not respond within 28 days, the authority can assume they have no comments to make.

The purpose of giving the Commission early warning in this way is to ensure that they know of any application that touches on the top 6% of our listed buildings – those in Grades I and II*. This has two advantages:

1. It means the Commission can try to influence the developer and the planning authority before the decision stage is reached: this may mean that the application can be modified in such a way as to make it more acceptable to all parties, with the saving of much time and temper on all sides.
2. If the Commission's powers of persuasion fail, they have the opportunity to make representations to the Secretary of State that the case should be called in for his decision.

The Commission thus have two bites of the cherry; but it is worth emphasizing that they only enjoy this privilege in relation to proposals to demolish, alter or extend Grade I or II* buildings. And planning authorities are not required to wait until they have heard from the Commission before determining the application, nor indeed to pay the slightest heed to what the Commission say if they do not wish to. Only the notification itself is a statutory requirement.

The only exception in this respect is Greater London. When the Greater London Council was abolished on 1 April 1986, English Heritage took over its Historic Buildings Division and its powers in relation to the London Boroughs. Section 14 of the 1990 Act requires London Borough Councils to notify English Heritage of any application for listed building consent which they do not determine to refuse, and thus provides that the last word on determination should rest with English Heritage. However, in 1993 the Government backed proposals for English Heritage to transfer responsibility for consent applications involving Grade II listed buildings to the London boroughs. English Heritage are now negotiating agreements with the individual boroughs to this end.

Notification of the Commission and the national amenity societies is fairly straightforward. Notifications to the Secretary of State are not. Up until 1987, the distinction between those applications which had to be notified and those which did not was defined in terms of grade and whether the application was to demolish or not. Now it is a good deal more complex. The growing numbers of listed buildings that resulted from the national resurvey meant that there was an increased strain on planning authorities. Circular 8/87 thus set out a revised direction which was aimed at reducing the number of cases that needed to be referred to the Secretary of State with consequent savings to authorities' budgets.

The Secretary of State has directed that where a planning authority are proposing to grant listed building consent, they should notify him of their intention unless the application refers to the demolition, alteration or extension of a Grade II building. But lest it be thought that the Secretary of State was relinquishing all control over 94% of our listed building stock, the direction lists eight exceptions. Applications falling into one or more of these categories and involving Grade II listed buildings must therefore still be referred to the Secretary of State. The eight categories are as follows.

1. Applications involving the total demolition of a principal building (defined in the direction as a building shown in the statutory list but not including a curtilage building).
2. Applications involving the total demolition of a curtilage building where it is specifically mentioned in the list description (unless it is expressly stated that it is not of special interest).
3. Applications to demolish part of a principal building, where the cubic content, taken together with that of any other part of the building demolished since listing took place, exceeds 10% of the cubic content of the building when listed. An exception is made to the exception, so to speak, in the case of pre-1914 buildings where the part to be demolished has been built since that date; and in the case of post-1948 extensions on inter-war buildings:

consent for partial demolition in these cases can take place without reference to the Secretary of State.

4. Applications for the total demolition of an elevation of a principal building.
5. Applications for the demolition of 'substantially all of the interior' of a principal building.
6. Applications for the partial or total demolition of any object or structure fixed to a principal or curtilage building provided that it is mentioned in the list description (again, unless it is mentioned simply to record that it has no special interest).
7. Applications for total or partial demolition which are made within five years of the Secretary of State determining a previous such application.
8. Applications affecting buildings which have received or which are the subject of applications for grant under the Historic Buildings & Ancient Monuments Act 1953.

Proposals are in train to simplify this direction.

In Greater London, the position is slightly different, in that the Commission already has a power of control which is in addition to that exercised by the London Boroughs. Accordingly, the Secretary of State has relinquished the right to see applications affecting the alteration or extension of any grade of listed building, as well as those concerned with the demolition of Grade II listed buildings (the same eight categories of exception apply).

Notifications to the Secretary of State are sent to the Regional Offices of the Department of the Environment, and the application will normally be accompanied by the authority's reasons for being disposed to grant consent, the representations that have been received and by photographs. The Secretary of State will then decide whether to call the case in for his own decision. There is no hard-and-fast set of rules by which he will be guided, but among the things normally considered are:

- the importance of the building and the effect the proposals in the application will have on it;
- the expressed views of the national amenity societies;
- the views of English Heritage;
- the strength of local opinion.

Of these, the views of English Heritage are the most important, since they are the Secretary of State's advisers. But it is important to stress that their role is simply to advise: and the Secretary of State is not bound to accept what they recommend.

In addition to exercising the power of call-in (which will normally be followed by a public local inquiry conducted by an inspector), the Secretary of State also has a role in determining appeals (see section 6.7) and in acting effectively as a referee where a London Borough is unwilling to accept the Commission's direction to refuse consent. The Secretary of State has a difficult balance to keep. Listing by definition is a special form of control, and this suggests that the determination of consents should not be left entirely to local planning authorities. On the other hand, the number of listed buildings has quadrupled in the past 25 years, and this has meant a great deal of extra work for local authorities: obviously if they are to refer a certain proportion to the Secretary of State, this is going to involve a certain amount of paperwork, a certain amount of administration and, in the natural way of things, a certain amount of delay. This labyrinthine direction is the Government's attempt to reduce the burden on local planning authorities. An extra complicating factor has been the emergence of English Heritage, which was created among many other things to give the Secretary of State independent and expert advice, and which has rightly been trying to create a role for itself since its establishment.

The local planning authority have eight weeks in which to decide an application for consent. The period may be extended by agreement between the authority and the applicant, but the applicant otherwise is entitled to assume a deemed refusal if he/she has not had a decision from the authority (or has not been notified that the application has been referred to the Secretary of State) by the end of the eight week period. The applicant can then exercise his/her right of appeal, just as if the application had been refused. The position here is exactly analogous to that for planning applications, and allows applications for planning permission and listed building consent to be considered in step.

Applications for consent will normally be considered by the planning authority's officials, who will make a recommendation to the relevant Council committee. Most Councils have a system of delegated powers which allows minor decisions to be taken by officers alone: but this does not usually apply to consent applications. The decision is taken in almost every case by the planning or development committee (the name varies between authorities) subject only to the directions of the Commission (in London) and notification to the Secretary of State. The committee will consider not only their officers' views but those of the Commission, the national amenity societies and local residents in coming to their decision. As with our planning system, much of the apparent slowness of the regime is in fact a reflection of the democratic nature of the decision-taking. That is not to say that every decision will be to the tastes of the electorate to whom the planning committee members are responsible; but it does mean everyone will have their say and that their views will be taken into account.

Once consent has been granted, work can normally proceed (unless conditions attached to the consent specify any preliminary action). In the case of consent to demolish a listed building, however, notification must be sent to the Royal Commission on the Historical Monuments of England. This is done both by the authority and by the applicant, for whom the authority will enclose a form for forwarding to the Commission with their decision letter. The Commission have one month from the date of the grant of the consent to enter the building to record it before it is demolished. If they do not wish to exercise this right, they will normally tell the holder of the consent.

6.4
Criteria for granting consent

The criteria by which both local planning authorities and the Secretary of State decide applications for consent are set out in section 16(2) of the 1990 Act. The subsection states

In considering whether to grant listed building consent for any works the local planning authority or the Secretary of State shall have special regard to the desirability of preserving the building or its setting or any features of special architectural or historical interest which it possesses.

This is the starting point. PPG15 fills out the criteria. It makes an important distinction between planning and listed building control: for where in planning there is a presumption in favour of development, the presumption in listed building control is in favour of preservation. The onus is accordingly placed on the applicant to show that there is a good case for what he/she is proposing. As the PPG states (paragraph 3.3), listed buildings represent a finite resource and an irreplaceable asset. Applicants for consent accordingly will need to demonstrate why the proposed works are desirable or necessary.

The PPG goes on (paragraph 3.5) to provide four general criteria for considering consent applications.

1. The importance of the building in terms of its intrinsic architectural and historic interest and rarity. Clearly a I or II* grading is a good cue but does not undermine the importance of the 94% of listed buildings that are listed Grade II.
2. The particular physical features of the building which justify its listing. The fact that these may not feature in the list description is not conclusive, given the sketchy nature of many of these.
3. The building's setting and its contribution to the local scene.
4. The extent to which the proposed work will bring substantial benefits for the community, in particular by contributing to the economic regeneration of the area or the enhancement of its environment.

The PPG lays great stress – and quite rightly – on the importance of securing the upkeep of listed buildings by keeping them in active use. It recognizes the difficulties that face developers and planning authorities in striking the right balance between the claims of conservation and the necessity of physical adaptation, and as a guiding principle it suggests the aim should be to identify the optimum viable use that is compatible with the fabric, interior and setting of the building. Where a building is so sensitive that it cannot sustain the alterations needed to make it economically viable, the circular suggests that community or charitable ownership may be the key.

The PPG goes on to deal with alterations and extensions. The general criteria will apply, but the type of balance needed for judging the desirability of a new use again is relevant. The PPG helpfully follows Circular 8/87 in devoting a whole annex to technical advice from English Heritage on alterations and extensions.

Finally in this section the PPG turns to the issue of demolitions. It has strong words to say. It makes clear that the destruction of historic buildings is very seldom needed in the interests of good planning and is more often the result of neglect or of a failure to find a suitable new use. Paragraph 3.17 spells out that the Secretary of State would look upon consent for the demolition of any Grade I or II* building as wholly exceptional, and that consent for the demolition of any listed building would only be granted where there was clear and convincing evidence that all reasonable efforts to sustain an existing use or to find a new one had been exhausted and that community or charitable ownership was not an option. The PPG does however allow for consent where demolition would produce benefits to the community which would decisively outweigh the loss resulting from the demolition. But there are words of discouragement for any demolition proposals coming from a developer arguing that repair or reuse were less attractive economically.

In addition to the general criteria set out at 3.5, the PPG lists three further considerations that the Secretary of State thinks are relevant to consent applications involving demolition.

1. The condition of the building, and the cost of repairing and maintaining it in relation to its importance and the value derived from its continued use. Any assessment will be based on long-term assumptions and should take account of possible tax allowances and exemptions, and grants. In cases of deliberate neglect, less weight will be given to repair costs.
2. The efforts that have been made to keep the building in use. These should include the offer of an unrestricted freehold on the open market at a realistic price.
3. The merits of alternative proposals for the site. The PPG seems to be pointing here towards the similar criterion which applies under the general set of considerations that apply for consent applications. The architectural merits of proposed replacement buildings are cited as not being in themselves justification for the demolition of a listed building – though they may be one consideration.

6.5
Problems with consent

Problems of definition can sometimes arise in determining where consent is necessary. What for instance constitutes an alteration to a listed building? Once upon a time the repainting of facades was not regarded by the Department as an alteration, and so did not require consent. But then in 1987, in the case of *Royal Borough of Windsor and Maidenhead* v. *Secretary of State for the Environment and Others*, it was held by the Court that repainting could constitute an alteration requiring consent if it affected the character of a listed building as one of special architectural or historic interest.

The most common source of dissent is in the matter of curtilage controls. As we have seen, listed building consent is required for

Saved by spot-listing: *top*: Wimbledon Town Hall (1928); and *bottom*: Raynes Park Methodist Church (1914)

works affecting any pre-1948 curtilage buildings. But how is the curtilage defined? There is no definition in the Act, and in spite of pressure on them to do so, the Department refused to define the curtilage of listed buildings in the course of the resurvey. This is hardly surprising as it is unlikely that there could be a hard and fast definition: without a scrutiny of the title deeds of every listed building owner's property, it would be impossible to define curtilage in any way (and even the deeds would be imperfect as they often relate to land which is quite outside the immediate vicinity of the listed building). Nor have the Courts been very helpful. In the case of *Attorney-General ex rel Sutcliffe* v. *Calderdale Borough Council* (the so-called Calderdale case), the Courts held that a row of unlisted mill cottages were within the curtilage of the listed mill despite the fact that they were only linked by a bridge. But in a rating case, *Debenhams plc* v. *Westminster City Council*, the House of Lords found that an unlisted portion of Debenhams store had not been listed by virtue of its being linked to a listed portion by a footbridge over a street and a tunnel under it. But it is to the Courts we must turn for such advice as there is. The most helpful definition of curtilage was given in the Scottish Court of Session in 1950, when it was held that

the ground which is used for the comfortable enjoyment of a house or other building may be regarded in law as being within the curtilage of that house or building and thereby an integral part of the same although it has not been marked off or enclosed in any way. It is enough that it serves the purpose of the house or building in some necessary or reasonably useful way.

In the Calderdale case, Lord Justice Stephenson suggested three factors which should be taken into account in defining whether a building lies within the curtilage of another:

1. the physical layout of the listed building and the structure;
2. their ownership, past and present;
3. their use or function, past and present.

PPG15 provides a supplementary and overlapping set of tests (paragraph 3.55):

1. the historical independence of the building;
2. the physical layout of the principal and other buildings;
3. the ownership of the buildings now and at the time of listing;
4. whether the structure forms part of the land;
5. the use and function of the buildings, and whether a building is ancillary or subordinate to the principal building.

In the majority of cases, it will be clear enough whether curtilage controls apply and consent is required. But in cases of dispute, the planning authority should be consulted; and if satisfaction is still not achieved, the only recourse is the Courts.

The third type of case which causes controversy is that concerning statues and sculptures inside houses. In recent years, when architectural salvage has become quite an industry, this has become an important issue. The most common type of case is that of a statue placed in a niche in a wall or on a staircase. Is it a chattel which the owner can remove at will? Or is it part of the interior fabric of the building requiring listed building consent before it can be taken away? Section 1(5) of the Act defines a listed building as including 'any object or structure fixed to the building'. Paragraphs 3.31 and 3.32 of PPG15 helpfully set out the current position, which as with curtilage has largely been defined by case law. The word 'fixed' generally connotes some degree of physical annexation to the building, with the intention of making the object integral to it. So a chimney-piece or wall panelling would normally count as fixed: works of art placed in a building to be enjoyed in their own right would not. But there are two important riders to this definition. First, freestanding objects such as statues may be counted as fixtures if they were put in place as part of an original overall architectural design. Second, items fixed to the building which were not part of the original design may fall outside listed building control, as the extraordinary *Orchardleigh* case demonstrated. This concerned a large Somerset country house, from which a fender and an overmantel had been removed without consent. The court ruled that this was within the law, as the prosecution had not been able to show that either object had been put in place at the time the house was built.

6.6
Conditions

Conditions can be attached to listed building consents in just the same way that they can in the case of planning permissions. In fact section 18 of the 1990 Act requires that at least one condition is attached to the consent, namely one relating to the time limit in which the consent may be exercised (the normal maximum period allowed is five years, again, exactly analogous to the position with planning permissions). Rather oddly, section 17(1) not only makes provision for the grant of conditional consents but goes on to spell out the sort of conditions that may be included: these include provision for conditions covering the preservation of particular features of the building, making good any damage to the building caused by the work carried out to it and the use of original materials.

Section 17(2) also makes provision for conditions allowing for the later approval of specified details. Finally, section 17(3) allows for the use of a condition on consents for demolition specifying that the listed building shall not be pulled down before a contract for the redevelopment of the site has been signed and planning permission for the new work has been granted. This is designed to avoid ugly gaps appearing where demolition is not followed by immediate redevelopment of the site.

A further attempt to speed up the consent process is contained in section 19, which permits planning authorities or the Secretary of State to vary or revoke conditions without forcing the applicant to lodge a fresh application. This covers the sort of position that can arise when work in progress reveals problems or information about the building that were not envisaged when the consent was granted. The power also enables fresh conditions to be added to the consent if circumstances warrant this.

6.7
Appeals

Applicants for listed building consent may appeal to the Secretary of State in three cases:

1. if their application is refused;
2. if their application is granted subject to conditions (in both instances, the planning authority's notice of refusal must state the reasons for their decision);
3. if the application is not decided within eight weeks or such longer period as the applicant and the planning authority have agreed.

The procedure for appealing is exactly the same as that for a normal planning appeal, and the same sorts of regulations and rules apply. If a concurrent planning application is also the subject of an appeal, then the two will normally be considered together.

Normally, it should be possible to decide minor appeals by means of written representations, that is to say, an exchange of representations from the planning authority (who will include objectors' comments) and the applicant. This is usually the cheapest and quickest means of determining an appeal. For more controversial cases, particularly where a number of parties may be involved, a hearing is an option: this is a relatively new procedure that avoids the formal and quasi-legal atmosphere of a public local inquiry but which allows for face-to-face exchanges of views. In complex or very controversial cases, a full-blown inquiry, however, is inevitable. It is normally costly, particularly if the parties are represented by counsel, and may take a little time to arrange. In all cases, the appeal will be entertained by an inspector appointed by the Secretary of State, and in most instances he will also be responsible for taking the decision. In more controversial cases, however, including all those relating to Grade I and II* buildings, he will present a recommendation, and the decision will be taken by the Secretary of State.

6.8
Demolition: the statistics

It may be instructive to pause at this point to consider the statistics for the demolition of listed buildings. One of the most quoted figures in the first months of European Architectural Heritage Year (1975) was that for every day of the year, one listed building was being demolished. One might think that with the tremendous growth in listed buildings as a result of the resurvey, this trend would have increased. But not a bit of it. Paradoxically, but very encouragingly, the numbers of buildings demolished have actually gone down. In 1977 (250 000 listed buildings) 306 consents for demolition were given; in 1988 (427 000 listed buildings) 185 consents were given; and in 1994/95 (500 000 listed buildings) just 92 were given.

The loss of even 64 listed buildings will seem a lot to the conscientious conservationist: but some of these will be comparatively minor structures, such as walls and gateposts, which, while every effort should be made to preserve them, are yet not exactly in the superleague of Grade I. On the whole, local planning authorities exercise an excellent stewardship over the listed buildings in their areas. Listing is not and has never been intended to be a guarantee of preservation at all costs. That the haemorrhage of listed buildings is so small is a matter for quiet but not complacent satisfaction.

6.9
Prosecution and enforcement

Nevertheless, there is a minority of unscrupulous owners and developers who carry out work without consent. Figures are difficult to assess, not least because the number of cases that reach the stage of prosecution in the Courts is tiny. Much depends on the vigilance of local authority planning enforcement officers – and indeed the general public – and in some cases the damage is put right without recourse to prosecution.

The offence of carrying out works of demolition, alteration or extension to a listed building without the necessary consent is one of strict liability: that is to say, it is not necessary for the prosecution to prove that the defendant knew that the building concerned was a listed one. As we have seen, the Department of National Heritage goes to some lengths to inform owners as soon as their properties have been listed: and in addition, planning authorities are required to serve a formal notice of listing on owners. But even in the best-run world, letters and notices would not always reach those to whom they were addressed, and a common defence is that the owner (or as frequently their contractors) did not know that the building concerned was listed. It is up to the Courts to decide whether they believe this, and if so how much they will mitigate the penalty.

One defence that has always been open to those demolishing a building without consent has been that this course was necessary in the interests of health and safety because the building was in a dangerous condition. It is important to underline that to demolish a building in such circumstances does not remove the fact that an offence has been committed. It simply states that the health and safety argument is a defence in any proceedings taken subsequently. And quite rightly, most of us would say. But there was a feeling shared by Government and conservationists alike that this defence was sometimes being abused; that not every developer was being entirely scrupulous in the application of what should have been a defence only of the last resort. The Housing & Planning Act 1986 accordingly strengthened the provisions considerably in an effort to remove any existing loopholes. In mounting a defence on 'dangerous structure' grounds, it is now necessary to prove all of the following matters:

1. that the works were urgently necessary in the interests of safety or health or for the preservation of the building;
2. that it was not practicable to secure safety and health or to preserve the building by repair works or works affording temporary support or shelter;
3. that the works carried out were the minimum recourse immediately necessary;
4. that notice in writing justifying in detail the carrying out of the works was given to the local planning authority as soon as was reasonably practicable.

Prosecutions for listed building offences can be started by anybody. In practice, it is normally the Secretary of State (through the Crown Prosecution Service) or the local planning authority who take offenders to Court, but occasionally a vigilant amenity society is involved. There are doubts over whether English Heritage has the legal power to carry out this sort of work, but the Government are hoping to clarify the position in new legislation.

At present, the maximum fine that can be imposed upon summary conviction is £5000 with three months' imprisonment as an alternative or an addition. In the latter case, the Courts are required to have regard to the financial benefit accruing to the guilty party as a result of the offence.

So much for what the law prescribes. There is nothing wrong with the penalties specified. They can be draconian, and one can but speculate what one well-publicized case of an offender cooling his heels in gaol for a few months would do to deter other potential offenders. Unfortunately, as with so many such environmental offences, the Courts, and in particular magistrates courts, seem reluctant to impose the maximum penalties allowed even in the most serious cases. A fine of a few hundred or even a few thousand pounds is scarcely likely to deter a builder or a developer who may stand to make many tens of thousands by clearing an awkwardly-sited listed building out of the way. But such penalties are likely to deter planning authorities or private individuals from launching prosecutions: and this could well be the reason why so few cases reach the Courts each year.

Classic 20th century designs: *top*: Odeon cinemas; and *bottom*: London tube stations by Charles Holden.

Most prosecutions are under section 9 of the 1990 Act. But we should note that it is also possible to prosecute under section 59 in respect of offences causing or likely to cause damage to listed buildings (the penalty here is £1000); and that section 59 also extends to buildings which are the subject of building preservation notices.

Rather than prosecute, most planning authorities prefer to rely on listed building enforcement notices. These are analogous to cnforcement notices used in ordinary development control cases, except that there is no time limit on the period in which the notice can be served. The notice may require the building:

1. to be returned to its former state;
2. to be brought to the state it would have been if the terms of any consent granted had been observed;
3. to be subject to such other works as the notice specifies to alleviate the effect of the unauthorized work.

A fine of up to £5000 on summary conviction (and unlimited on indictment) may be imposed for contraventions of an enforcement notice, and there is the option of a further fine of £200 a day in the event that the offence continues. An appeals system operates, again in parallel with those for ordinary enforcement notices. As with appeals against the refusal of consent, it is possible to argue against the imposition of an enforcement notice on the grounds that the building in respect of which it has been served is not of special architectural or historic interest and should be removed from the list.

One important distinction from the planning system does relate to the question of offences. In planning law, it is not an offence to carry out work without planning permission but it is to carry out work in defiance of an enforcement notice. This permits the planning authority in considering enforcement action to ask themselves whether they would have granted permission for the development had it been sought. In listed building legislation, no such provision exists. It is now possible under section 8(3) to obtain a consent even though the works to which it relates have been completed. But this is not retrospective. The consent covers the works from the time it is given: it does not alter the fact that an offence has been committed by carrying out the work without consent in the first place, and the offender is accordingly still liable to prosecution.

6.10
Purchase notices and compensation

If listed building consent is refused, or granted subject to conditions, it is open to the owner to serve a purchase notice on the planning authority requiring them to acquire his/her interest in the land. For this to succeed, the owner must show that the land has become incapable of reasonably beneficial use in its existing condition and that the refusal of consent, or the conditions attaching to the consent, has prevented a reasonably beneficial use being created for the land. These tests, which are set out in section 32 of the 1990 Act, are stiff and intentionally so.

The planning authority have three months in which to respond to the notice, and if they do not agree to acquire the land, they must refer the case to the Secretary of State for determination. In addition to confirming or rejecting the purchase notice, the Secretary of State has the right to grant a listed building consent, or to amend the conditions, if it is considered to be expedient.

Under section 27 of the 1990 Act, a local planning authority may be liable to pay compensation if the Secretary of State either on appeal or on a called-in application refuses consent for the alteration or extension of a listed building (but not for its demolition). However, the authority is only liable if the works do not constitute development or if they are covered by permitted development rights in a General Development Order; and only then if the owner's interest in the land is less than it would have been if the consent had been granted unconditionally.

This provision broadly follows the compensation payable in ordinary planning cases in similar circumstances. It ensures that an owner is compensated for work which in normal circumstances he/she would be able to carry out were it not for the restrictions imposed by listing. On the face of it, the fact that a planning authority have to pay out because of a decision taken by the Secretary of State seems unfair: but in fact it ensures that compensation is not payable simply because the planning authority have refused consent or granted it only conditionally – the case must go to appeal so that the Secretary of State can make a final determination before the question of compensation arises. The sort of case that could arise would be where consent is refused for interior alterations (since this does not constitute development); or where the refusal of consent confounds the permitted development rights to extend domestic or industrial premises which are covered in the General Development Order. But in each case, it will be necessary to show that the value of the property is less than it would have been if consent had been granted.

6.11
Applications by local authorities

So far, we have discussed applications for listed building consent as if they all come from private individuals or companies. In fact of course they do not. Applications for listed building consent from local authorities are particularly sensitive because as local custodians of the heritage they must be seen to set a good example. Departmental Circulars and ministerial speeches regularly encourage local authorities to take good or better care of their listed building stock. Section 82 of the 1990 Act requires all local authorities to make their own applications for listed building consent direct to the Secretary of State (in fact to one of his regional offices). Applications from County Councils must be made via District Councils so that they, as the normal planning authority, may comment upon them.

6.12
The position of the churches

Under section 60(1), an ecclesiastical building which is for the time being used for ecclesiastical purposes is exempt from listed building control. This is the so-called ecclesiastical exemption. It is said to have its origins in an agreement between the Government and the then Archbishop of Canterbury in 1913. But it came to apply to all Christian churches, so weakening control in a significant category of heritage buildings. After lengthy discussions over a period of years, the position was clarified and made more restrictive in the Ecclesiastical Exemption (Listed Buildings & Conservation Areas) Order 1994.

The Order did two things. First, it specified the religious denominations to which the exemption applies.These are churches which have their own internal systems for determining what are *de facto* consent applications and whose procedures have satisfied the

Department of National Heritage as to their rigour. The six churches specified are:

1. the Church of England;
2. the Church in Wales;
3. the Roman Catholic Church;
4. the Methodist Church;
5. the Baptist Union of Great Britain and the Baptist Union of Wales;
6. the United Reformed Church.

All other denominations and faiths, including the Jews, Muslims and Hindus and other Christian denominations, are now subject to the full range of listed building controls.

Secondly, the Order prescribes clearly the works that are exempt from control. These are proposals affecting:

1. church buildings used primarily for worship;
2. objects or structures within the church building;
3. objects or structures fixed to the exterior of church buildings (unless themselves listed);
4. objects or structures within the curtilage of the church buildings (again, unless themselves listed).

A guidance note from DNH *The Ecclesiastical Exemption – what it is and how it works* sets out details of the way the exemption works in particular cases.

6.13
The Crown and the Historic Buildings and Monuments Commission

Although Crown buildings can be listed, the Crown does not need listed building consent for their alteration, extension or demolition. However, since the Government Estate is so large, the Crown will consult local planning authorities about their proposals and the procedure is laid down in Circular 18/84. Essentially, the authority is asked to treat the consultation as if it were a formal application, and they should advertise and notify the proposals in the normal way. In the event of there being a disagreement between the developing Department and the planning authority, the matter will be referred to the Department of the Environment. They may solicit an exchange of written representations; they may hold an informal meeting of the interested parties; or they may hold a non-statutory public inquiry. If it is decided to proceed with demolition, then the developing Department will give the Royal Commission one month's notice in the normal way so that it has an opportunity to record the building in question.

The Crown may now also apply to planning authorities for listed building consent if they so wish. The provision, introduced in the Town & Country Planning Act 1984 (and now contained in section 84 of the 1990 Act), enables the Crown to dispose of land with the benefit of consent in respect of any listed buildings on it. The Act similarly permitted the Crown to apply for planning permission in the same way. It is worth adding that, in 1993, the Government announced its intention to end the Crown's immunity from planning and conservation controls as soon as a legislative opportunity could be found.

As far as work to listed buildings by the Historic Buildings and Monuments Commission is concerned, the Secretary of State has directed in paragraph 102 of Circular 8/87 that all applications should be made to him. Authorities are asked to advertise such applications, and to forward any representations they receive to the Department's regional office.

6.14
Conclusion

The listed building consent system is only just over 25 years old, and yet it has already become a complex branch of planning law. This is in part because of the conflicting pressures of conservation and redevelopment, and the need to strike a balance – and the right balance – very speedily.

The result has been that, despite the important and emotive nature of the subject, there is in fact very little case law relating to listed building matters. The system is not straightforward, but it seems to work. It is considerably more complicated than most western European legislation on conservation, but it works for the best possible reason: the majority of the population seem to want it to work. Despite the occasional grumbles of listed building owners and developers, the fact that we are losing so little of our architectural heritage – while so much is being added to it – is surely a sign that the system of control is welcomed and is enforced fairly and firmly by local planning authorities, by the Commission and by the Secretary of State. Complacent? Perhaps. The proof of the pudding in this case is the effectiveness of the legislation in protecting so much of our listed heritage and allowing sensitive adaptation to take place where possible to enable an old building to enjoy a new lease of life. The listed building control system has a good track record. Would it be possible to devise an alternative that would please so many different interests so well? I honestly doubt it.

Chapter 7

CONSERVATION AREAS

There are now over 8000 conservation areas in England, and smaller numbers in Scotland and Wales. Since their introduction in 1967, when just four were designated as the first group, they have become a cornerstone of conservation policy in this country. They contain an estimated 1.3 million buildings – something over 4% of the nation's total building stock.

Conservation areas bridge the gap between the special controls that apply to listed buildings and the normal forms that apply to most development. Conservation areas have adopted certain aspects of the listed building regime – notably in the controls over demolition – and have also added their own gloss to normal planning controls. This reflects their status as a second tier form of statutory protection over buildings which, while not good enough to be listed in their own right, nonetheless have a special value when considered as part of an area.

7.1
Definition

The key word here is area. Conservation areas are defined (section 69 of the 1990 Act) as areas

of special architectural or historic interest the character or appearance of which it is desirable to preserve or enhance

As with listing, there is no statutory definition of what constitutes this special interest, and the guidance of the Secretary of State is couched in even more general terms than the 'Principles of Selection' for listing. Paragraph 4.4 of PPG15 makes some suggestions, but these are cast in very general terms. The paragraph states that certain aspects will almost always form the basis for assessing special character – topography of the area, its historical development, the construction materials used, and the quality and interrelationships of its buildings and of its trees and open spaces. The purpose is to give a very wide discretion as to what can be included in a conservation area. This leads to the curious anomaly, for instance, that the Secretary of State has not suggested any date criteria similar to those applicable in the case of listing. No Thirty Year Rule here! And since the Act refers to special architectural *or* historic interest as the criterion for designation, it would be, strictly speaking, possible to designate a modern shopping centre provided that it was felt to be of good architectural quality. And why not?

One of the main points of difficulty that arises in connection with conservation areas is the problem of deciding when designation or listing for group value is the right course. This is one of those nice semantic points that occasionally exercise conservationists. Buildings are listed for their group value when they possess special interest by virtue of their interrelationship. The usual example that is quoted is a terrace of modest Georgian houses: their interiors may have lost all interest as a result of alterations or decay; but their facade may just possess enough special interest for the houses to be listed if the unity of its original composition has been preserved. The same may go for modest vernacular houses, insufficiently distinguished by themselves for listing but forming a little group which does satisfy the stringent criteria for listing when considered together. Conservation area status is appropriate where the buildings are not themselves of special interest (although some may be listed) and where the special interest belongs to the area as a whole. In these cases, the buildings may each make a contribution to the quality of the conservation area, but other factors will be relevant too – for example, the configuration of the streets, the roofscape or the positioning of a central feature, such as a church or a market-hall.

In general, conservation areas are a lot larger than the groups covered by listing; but there are grey areas. Model villages established by benevolent employers in the last century are an example. They have some interest as early examples of town planning and as an important part of our economic and social history, although this may not always add up to their being listable. What then? Should they be listed for their group value, since undoubtedly the fact that, although modest, they are all located together gives them architectural interest? Or should they simply be designated as conservation areas (always provided they satisfy the broad criteria of paragraph 4.4)? The answer is something for Government, central and local, to decide for themselves, with the advice if necessary of the Commission.

In practice, conservation areas cover a wide variety of forms of special interest. Historic town centres were for the most part designated long ago. Most of our older villages now have their central areas designated, and Victorian suburbs like Bedford Park and Merton Park in London have also been included. Now the talk is of designating areas of the better inter-war housing. Some of the 'homes fit for heroes' built by local authorities after the First World War have already been the subject of designation orders, and now a few authorities are considering whether this protection should be extended to the estates of Tudorbethan gems so scorned by some and so well-loved by others.

One footnote must be appended to this section on 'outstanding' conservation areas. This was a description applied by Government to distinguish those areas whose lucky inhabitants were eligible to receive what became known as 'section 10 grants' under the Town & Country Planning (Amendment) Act 1972. The distinction was not applied after 1980. About 550 conservation areas had been designated 'outstanding' up to that time and the term is still heard. It has no meaning in law, although no doubt this official recognition, albeit rather out of date now, could still be deployed in arguments for or against a proposal affecting the area. Even at the time it was given, the term was slightly misleading, as it was not a description given following any systematic survey of all conservation areas in the country. But that does not, and perhaps should not, stop local pride from quoting the designation.

7.2
Designation

Section 69 of the 1990 Act places a duty on local authorities to determine which parts of their areas possess special architectural or historic interest and to designate these as conservation areas. The duty is similar to that placed on the Secretary of State in relation to listing buildings but it has not been tested in the Courts. It should be clear, however, that there is no overriding obligation on a local authority to designate conservation areas; they are simply obliged to consider the possibility, and if they conclude that there are no areas of special interest, then they are right not to make any designations. In practice, every authority in England has now made at least one designation, and most localities have a number of conservation areas within their boundaries.

The vast majority of designations are made by district planning authorities and the London boroughs. The Secretary of State has a power (i.e. a discretion) to make designations, but he has never used it and PPG15 makes it clear that he would do so only very exceptionally. County planning authorities also have a power of designation, but they must consult the relevant district before exercising this. In London, the Greater London Council's powers of designation have been taken over by English Heritage, and they are again expected to use this in consultation with the London Boroughs.

Once a council decides to designate an area as a conservation area, the designation takes effect from the date of the resolution. Careful definition by reference to a map is the usual course. Odd effects can occur otherwise. I once lived in a property where the front garden was in a village conservation area but the house itself was not!

The Council are obliged to do three things upon designation. First, they must put notice of the designation in the London Gazette and in at least one local newspaper. Secondly, they must register the designation as a land charge, which is as near an official notification as some householders will get. Thirdly, they must inform the Secretary of State and the Commission of the designation. In practice, many local authorities will go rather farther than that and will circulate to all the properties within the newly-designated area a letter or a leaflet telling them what has occurred and what the effect of it will be for them. Many of these leaflets are well-produced, and by giving some of the history of the area and the reasons for designation may encourage local pride and an increased sense of local community. After all, the purpose of designation is to preserve and enhance, and the latter objective is made a lot easier when owners take pride not just in their own properties but in their local areas as well.

The Act deals with the question of de-designating a conservation area rather oddly.There is no specific provision to amend a conservation area's designation (as there is with the statutory list) or to reverse it entirely: but section 70(5) and (6) refer to the procedure to be followed in the event of a designation or a variation or cancellation of it. Until the law is tested in the Courts or is clarified by further legislation the validity of de-designation or amendment looks open to question.

7.3
General principles following designation

When a building is listed, the procedure is often (but not always rightly) seen as an end in itself to secure the building's protection. Conservation area designation, on the other hand, is not an end but a means to an end.The emphasis is on enhancement as well as preservation and statutory backing to this line, so far as the gamut of planning powers is concerned, is contained in the Act.

The general principle is that a conservation area should not be mummified by cocooning it from change. Paragraph 4.16 of PPG15 states that while conservation must be a major consideration (the use of the indefinite article is significant) this cannot take the form of preventing all new development, and that accordingly the emphasis will generally need to be on controlled and positive management of change. The important factor will be the extent to which any new development blends well with the area and fits in with its character. This will mean in some instances that planning authorities should insist on detailed planning applications where they might otherwise have been content to consider them in outline.

The importance of preservation and enhancement in conservation areas, and their precise interpretation, are questions that have been tested in the Courts. On the first issue, the 1988 case of *Steinberg and another* v. *the Secretary of State and another* was important. The court ruled that the question of preservation and enhancement was the key factor in considering any planning proposals affecting a conservation area; simply to say that the proposals would not harm the area was insufficient. This line is reflected in paragraph 4.19 of PPG15, where it is stated bluntly that any proposal conflicting with the objectives of preservation and enhancement is unlikely to secure planning permission.

On the second issue, the courts held in the case of *South Lakeland DC* v. *the Secretary of State for the Environment* that the Act does not require that conservation areas should be protected

Two conservation areas. These buildings are not listable but they help to give their streets a special character and appearance.

from all development that does not enhance or positively preserve. The objective of preservation can be met by development making a positive contribution to the area's character or appearance, or by development which leaves these features unharmed.

Preservation and enhancement are important: but what is the means for communicating to developers the policies that apply to conservation areas? We saw in section 6.2 the new importance that section 54A of the Town & Country Planning Act 1990 gives to the development plan. Since section 71 of the Planning (Listed Buildings & Conservation Areas) Act 1990 requires proposals for conservation to be published, the plan seems a natural vehicle. But the 1994 case of *R* v. the *Secretary of State for the Environment* ex parte *the Mayor & Burgesses of the London Borough of Islington* underlined both the Secretary of State's distaste for detailed policy statements in development plans and his right, under section 17 of the Town & Country Planning Act, to reject their inclusion. Nothing, however, prevents local planning authorities putting such statements in the form of supplementary planning guidance, and this is a course that many already take.

7.4
Article 4 directions and conservation areas

Article 4 directions allow planning authorities to remove a range of permitted development rights granted under the Town & Country Planning General Permitted Development and Development Procedure Orders. Most of these rights relate to small-scale developments – certain minor house extensions, roof alterations and the erection of gates and walls. In most areas, the Government seeks to lighten the load on both householders and other developers and the planning authority by granting a general planning permission. But equally Government recognizes that the unfettered exercise of these rights in environmentally sensitive cases could prove detrimental, and thus planning authorities are permitted to revoke them – in general, subject to the Secretary of State's consent – so requiring the developer to make a planning application in the normal way.

Planning authorities are able to make directions under Article 4 of the Permitted Development Order to remove permitted development rights in the case of listed buildings without reference to the

Secretary of State. In 1995, this right was extended to embrace some aspects of the external appearance of houses – together with gates, walls and fences – in conservation areas. But, in general, Article 4 directions will otherwise continue to require consent from the Secretary of State, although he has said that he will generally be sympathetic to approving Article 4 directions in conservation areas, provided that a special need for them can be shown. This would take the form, for instance, of an actual or potential threat to the area from the exercise of permitted development rights (`for instance, those allowed to householders and industrialists); or where a direction would help the planning authority in any positive programme of improvements for the area. Even in these cases, the emphasis will be on the minimum degree of extra control that is necessary.

The emphasis here, as elsewhere, is on using the existing armoury of development controls sensibly and sensitively in conservation areas. It is recourse to the épée rather than the bludgeon.

7.5
Control of demolition in conservation areas

So far we have covered the extension of the normal forms of development control to conservation areas. But the other side of this is the extension of the various forms of special control as well. Conservation areas were Johnny-come-latelies to the planning scene, and this meant that pieces of the existing legislation could be taken and adapted for them.

The most ambitious takeover of this kind was the extension of listed building controls to the demolition of unlisted buildings in conservation areas. Such was the extension of the long-standing provisions that up until 1984 the separate term conservation area consent was unknown. This particular extension of listed building controls was enacted originally in the Town & Country Amenities Act 1974, a measure that was passed as a private member's bill (but with Government support) between the two General Elections of that year. Overnight, as it were, the number of buildings protected by listed building controls must have doubled. Provision is now contained in sections 74–76 of the 1990 Act.

The requirement to obtain conservation area consent applies to all buildings in the conservation area except:

1. buildings which are themselves listed (which continue to be covered by the panoply of listed building controls);
2. ecclesiastical buildings which are for the time being used for ecclesiastical purposes;
3. buildings which are for the time being scheduled ancient monuments;
4. buildings which are the subject of a direction given by the Secretary of State under section 75(2) of the 1990 Act.

Buildings excluded under 1. are straightforward enough, since it would be invidious to apply to them a lesser degree of control than pertains to listed buildings outside conservation areas. Buildings excluded under 2. and 3. are simply enjoying a similar exemption to the one they have from listed building control under sections 60 and 61. The most significant category is that included in 4. Section 75(2) permits the Secretary of State to direct that the section shall not apply to such categories of building as he may specify, and although section 75(3) permits him to direct either local planning authorities generally or an individual authority, the direction that has been issued applies to all authorities. The terms of the direction do not make easy reading. But in broad terms, the requirement to seek conservation area consent is disapplied in the following types of case:

1. any building with a total cubic content not exceeding 115 cubic metres (this does not cover parts of a building) – so the demolition of a small part of a larger building will almost certainly require consent);
2. gates, walls, fences and railings less than a metre high where abutting on a highway, and less than two metres in all other cases (note: there are proposals in hand to remove this exemption);
3. any building used for agriculture or forestry and built since 1914;
4. parts of industrial buildings not exceeding 10% of the original cubic content of the whole building or 500 square metres of floor space, whichever is the greater;
5. buildings subject to a discontinuance order or an enforcement notice;
6. buildings due to be demolished as part of a binding planning agreement or as a condition of a planning permission
7. buildings which have been compulsorily purchased under the Housing Act 1985 or which are due to be demolished as a result of the Pastoral Measure 1983.

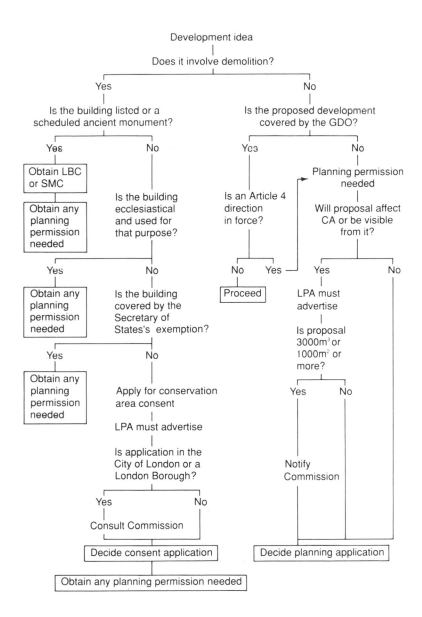

Figure 7.1 Work in conservation area.

The most important of these exemptions are those in 1. and 2., which ensure that there is no need to seek consent for the removal of small structures which might otherwise be a source of much paperwork both for their owners and for the local planning authority.

Applications for conservation area consent must be made to the local planning authority (the district, borough or London Borough Council). They are not required to notify the Secretary of State – unlike listed building consent cases – of the applications they receive. They must however apply to the Secretary of State when it is they themselves who are the applicants, and in the case of county councils they must route their applications through the district. In London, all applications for conservation area consent must be notified to English Heritage by the planning authority, which must also take account of their views in coming to a decision.

There is no prescribed form on which applications must be made, but most authorities will have their own. There is no fee to pay, but plans and drawings will need to accompany the application, and it would be as well to check with the planning authority exactly what information they will require. Since there is no requirement to notify the Secretary of State, there is every reason for consent applications to be dealt with expeditiously, and they will go to committee with other applications in the normal way.

But it is unlikely that the consent application will go to committee in isolation. Paragraph 4.29 of PPG15 spells out the Secretary of State's concern that unsightly gaps should not appear in conservation areas as a result of premature demolition: and so authorities are enjoined to grant consent only where there are detailed and acceptable plans for redevelopment (and presumably where they are satisfied that the demolition itself can be justified). The Secretary of State has the backing of the courts for this line. In the case of *Richmond upon Thames London Borough* v. *Secretary of State for the Environment* in 1979 it was held that the function of granting consent to demolish an unlisted building in a conservation area could not be divorced from the need to see what was being substituted and how it would fit into the area. Rather paradoxically, this has been slightly more difficult since 1980 when the Local Government Planning & Land Act ended the possibility of planning permissions in certain cases acting as consents: two separate decisions are now necessary, although they generally will proceed in tandem through the system.

Granting a planning permission for an acceptable new development is one thing: ensuring that it is carried through is another. paragraph 4.29 goes on to suggest that the proposed redevelopment should be the subject of a condition in the consent stating that demolition should not commence until a contract for redeveloping the site has been made.

Once the planning authority have received the application for conservation area consent, they will advertise it, and the representations they receive will be brought to councillors' attention and considered before a decision is made. But what else will influence the decision? This is where the most important distinction between listed building consent and conservation area consent is apparent. For where the intrinsic special architectural or historic interest of the building will be the criterion against which a listed building consent application will be tested, it is the effect on the conservation area as a whole that will concern those deciding whether to grant a conservation area consent. This means, for instance, that arguments about the interior of the building are unlikely to be relevant, since that plays no part in the look of the conservation area as a whole: it could well mean that some feature of minor architectural or historic interest, such as the line of a roof or the building's position in the street scene, is given new importance because of its effect on the character or appearance of the conservation area as a whole. The lay eye can be as useful here in making a judgment as the professional planner or the architectural historian.

We should also note here that the Act not only extends the listed building consent provisions to the demolition of unlisted buildings in conservation areas; it also extends a number of the other listed building provisions. These include the right to appeal against the refusal of consent; the enforcement provisions; and the provisions for revoking consent and in respect of purchase notices. The provision for the treatment of Crown land is also replicated in respect of conservation area consents.

The extension of control over the demolition of unlisted buildings in conservation areas has perhaps been the most significant advance in the heritage field since 1968. There have on occasion been accusations that individual planning authorities have misused their powers of designation in order to gain control over the demolition of buildings which are in no way listable and whose preservation would stand in the way of development proposals that they considered undesirable. Perhaps the accusations are true on occasion – their validity depends very much on your point of view.What is more difficult to dispute is the fact that many of our finest town centres and most beautiful areas have had their character preserved through the sensitive and sensible use of conservation area controls. Arguably it is one of the key components of our 'democratic' approach to the heritage which argues in favour of preserving the familiar and well-loved as much as the magnificent and grand.

7.6
Advertisement of applications in conservation areas

As we mentioned above, applications for conservation area consent must be advertised in the same way that listed building consent applications are. But the 1990 Act also requires applications for planning permission to be advertised under section 73. The practice of letting local residents know about possibly controversial and important applications is well-established in planning law – it applies to a whole list of so-called 'unneighbourly' developments. The extension of the practice from sensitive forms of development to sensitive locations like conservation areas was thus logical enough. The main difference is that the onus is on the planning authority rather than the applicant to advertise applications affecting conservation areas.The reason for this distinction is not immediately clear. One possible factor could be the practical one that advertisements for applications involving unneighbourly developments appear in newspapers in ones and twos; one could imagine that in some districts where there are a host of conservation areas the public notices columns of the local press would be full of owners' advertisements. By putting the duty on the planning authority, the notices can appear in consolidated and summary form – as indeed they normally do.

Whatever the reasoning, section 73 places a duty on the planning authority to publish a notice of all the applications they receive for planning permission for any development which in their opinion affects the character or appearance of a conservation area. The authority is required to publish the notice in a local newspaper circulating in the area in which the proposed development is sited; and to display it for seven days on or near the site itself. The notice must set out the nature of the development and name somewhere in the

Top: A school converted into flats in a conservation area. *Below*: Trees and open space can be almost as important as the buildings in a conservation area.

locality where a copy of the application and of all the plans and other documents submitted with it can be inspected. The planning authority are not allowed to decide the application until 21 days have elapsed both from the publication of the notice in the paper and the date on which the site notice was first displayed. The planning authority will then normally take into account all the representations they receive in response to the advertisements. As with listed buildings, there is of course no guarantee that they will abide by the spirit of public opinion!

The National Heritage Act 1983 inserted a new and rather ambitious statutory requirement. This was that planning authorities should send the Commission a copy of each notice they advertised. Since, as we saw in Chapter 6, the requirement to advertise applies to all those applications affecting the setting of a listed building as well as those affecting the character or appearance of a conservation area, it was not surprising that the Commission soon took an opportunity to seek to reduce their workload. Accordingly, the Secretary of State modified the requirement considerably. The Department had already in Circular 23/84 restricted the requirement in the case of conservation areas to some 500 named areas: now the provision was again recast. As a result, the Secretary of State has directed that only notices in respect of development of 3000 cubic metres or more, or 1000 square metres or more (including changes of use) should be notified to the Commission. There are proposals in hand slightly to amend these definitions. But it is worth noting that this requirement now applies to all conservation areas, and not just to the original named 500.

Consultation with the Commission continues to be the case for all cases where development would affect the character or appearance of grant-aided work in a conservation area, and the circular asks that this should take place at an early stage in drawing up the design proposals. Local authorities and Government Departments are also asked to notify the Commission of their proposals falling into all these categories.

7.7
Trees in conservation areas

The Town & Country Amenities Act 1974 not only introduced what we know now as conservation area consent. It also introduced a new and significant measure to protect trees in conservation areas. The existing legislation, contained in the 1971 Act, had already given local authorities the weapon of tree preservation orders. Now, the new Act introduced a further section into its predecessor, which recognized the important part that trees often play in enhancing the appearance of a conservation area.The new section is now sections 211–14 of the Town & Country Planning Act 1990. They require anyone proposing to do work in a conservation area on trees which were not already the subject of a tree preservation order to give the local planning authority six weeks notice of their intention before work is carried out. A register of such notifications has to be kept and the penalties for breach of the statutory requirement are similar to those for contravening a tree preservation order.

The law is slightly curious in that it does not allow for any specific application or the granting of any specific consent. The implication is that if the owner has heard nothing after six weeks, he/she may proceed; and that the local authority, if they want to protect the tree or control its lopping, should serve a proper preservation order upon it. Presumably there is nothing to stop the authority responding helpfully by return of post to the owner saying exactly what their intention is. But there is no provision for this in the Act.

There is inevitably a list of exemptions from the requirements of the Act. These are currently spelled out in the Town & Country Planning (Trees in Conservation Areas) (Exempted Cases) Regulations 1975. Broadly speaking, there are four categories:

1. cutting down, topping or lopping trees which are dying or dead or which have become dangerous;
2. various exemptions granted in connection with Forestry Commission schemes;
3. local planning authorities cutting down, topping or lopping trees on their own land;
4. cutting down, topping or lopping trees with diameters of less than 75 millimetres or 100 millimetres where the action is designed to improve the growth of other trees.

Although the last category does tempt muttered comments about the need for tape measures and a knowledge of Euclidean geometry, it does at least go a little way to help in distinguishing when a tree is not a tree so much as a bush (and vice versa!).

7.8
Advertisements in conservation areas

There are no special provisions for the control of advertisements in conservation areas. But once again, existing legislation is sufficient to cover the position if used sensitively. Successive Planning Acts have required the Secretary of State to make regulations to control the display of advertisements in the interests of amenity and safety, and from their inception these regulations have incorporated the idea of special controls for designated areas. The detailed regime is a complex one and has most recently been set out in the Town & Country Planning (Control of Advertisements) Regulations 1992. Certain categories of advertisement, for which there is 'deemed consent' elsewhere, are brought within local authority control in conservation areas, but in general, PPG15 asks authorities to use their powers flexibly, bearing in mind that many conservation areas are situated in commercial centres. Clearly no-one wants to introduce the roadside horrors of an American shopping mall into a historic area; but a flexible and sensitive approach on all sides should produce a satisfactory result. Some departmental advice on poster advertising in conservation areas is contained in PPG19.

7.9
Public participation: conservation area advisory committees

From their outset, successive Governments have encouraged public participation in the identification and enhancement of conservation areas. Section 71(1) places a duty on planning authorities to formulate and publish, from time to time, proposals for the preservation and enhancement of their conservation areas, and sections 71(2) and (3) require that such proposals should be submitted for consideration to a public meeting and that the authority should have regard to the views expressed at that meeting. This must be one of the few references in English law to public meetings coupled with a requirement to actually listen to what they say!

In addition, it is often helpful to discuss proposals and progress with amenity and residents groups and Chambers of Trade and Commerce. Many forward-thinking authorities do this very conscientiously with encouraging results. Local groups are usually pleased to be asked and glad to help. They can be helpful not just in providing the arm and leg power involved in helping to distribute leaflets to local residents and doing on occasion some elementary and necessary manual work but also in promoting goodwill among local people and traders. And any planning enforcement officer relies on local watchdogs to be his or her eyes and ears in watching for possible breaches of the planning regime. At local level, the work of amenity groups is as valuable as that of the national amenity societies to Government.

The most frequent formal expression of these groups' work is often to be found in conservation area advisory committees. These are purely voluntary and non-statutory local groups, whose establishment was first recommended in 1968 by Government. PPG15 (paragraph 4.13) again asks authorities to consider setting them up where none exist at present. The committees normally give their views on applications which would affect the character or appearance of a conservation area, as well as on more general policies in relation to conservation in the district. It is up to the authority to decide whether to set up one committee for the whole of their district or separate advisory committees for each conservation area or group of areas. The only suggestion the circular gives is that the membership of each committee should represent a cross-section of local opinion. The circular suggests that nominations should be sought from the national amenity societies, the Civic Trust and local history, civic and amenity societies. Council members could be on such committees, but normally the remainder of the membership might be made up of residents or tenants associations in an area predominantly of housing, or representatives of Chambers of Trade or Commerce in areas where there was a shopping or commercial centre. Many authorities find advisory committees very helpful, and a useful and fairly informal forum to discuss both their own proposals and any development plans that are either current or likely to be forthcoming.

7.10
Conclusion

Conservation areas have been one of the success stories of British conservation. Perhaps their main advantage is that they pass a degree of control, both in designation and the operation of controls, to local authorities and thus to local people themselves. It is certainly an oddity that while we insist on strict national criteria for the listing of buildings, so that the same standards apply in Penrith and Penzance (and of course in their Scottish and Welsh equivalents), the designation of conservation areas is left purely to local discretion.

Is this right? I believe it is. The listing of buildings can be considered as an imposition on their property rights by the individual citizen. Surely it is right that such a decision should be taken at national level, and that the Secretary of State should answer where necessary for individual listing decisions to Parliament. The designation of a conservation area does not impact on owners in quite the same way. Certainly they are likely to feel aggrieved if their applications for conservation area consent is refused – although they have of course a right of appeal to the Secretary of State. But where listing is aimed essentially at protection, which is ultimately a negative activity, designation is aimed – as the courts themselves have now emphasized – at preservation *and* enhancement. That is something that local people are best placed to undertake, calling on the help of national bodies where necessary. As we saw above, conservation areas are arguably part of the 'democratic' tradition of the British heritage. All those lesser buildings – which while not of listable quality are at least safe from uncontrolled demolition so long as they are in *areas* of special architectural or historic interest – are the stuff of our heritage because they are part of our surroundings and our everyday experience. That surely is a very important part of planning.

Chapter 8

ANCIENT MONUMENTS

Ancient monuments were the first historic items to be protected in this country. As we saw in Chapter 2, legislation for their preservation was first passed in the 1880s and predated that for historic buildings by some 60 years. Quite why the two codes have never been brought together is something of a mystery. Certainly to anyone from outside the United Kingdom it is odd that there are two quite separate pieces of legislation for ancient monuments and historic buildings. But perhaps it is the topsy-like growth of heritage legislation in this country which has produced the anomaly; and which will no doubt perpetuate it for years to come.

8.1
Definition

The definition of exactly what we are talking about is complex. First, we must define a monument. Then we have to define an ancient monument. Finally, we have to define a scheduled ancient monument – the type that enjoys statutory protection.

Although ancient monument legislation goes back to the last century, the key statute today is the Ancient Monuments & Archaeological Areas Act 1979. Section 61(7) of that Act defines a monument as:

(a) any building, structure or work, whether above above or below the surface of the land, and any cave or excavation;

(b) any site comprising the remains of any such building, structure or work or of any cave or excavation; and

(c) any site comprising, or comprising the remains of, any vehicle, vessel, aircraft, or other moveable structure or part thereof which neither constitutes nor forms part of any work which is a monument within paragraph (a) above;

and any machinery attached to a monument shall be regarded as part of the monument if it could not be detached without being dismantled.

This definition reveals three main differences between the legal view of a monument and a listed building:

1. the definition of a monument embraces a cave or an excavation which would not be eligible for listing (unless it was part of a building, like a cellar);
2. the definition of a monument refers to its site, as well as to the structure itself, so that the area of ground around the monument can be protected;
3. the monument may itself be a site comprising the remains of a moveable object, such as a vehicle or a piece of machinery.

This last difference is particularly worth highlighting, because a piece of machinery can be protected by scheduling where it cannot be covered by listing simply because it does not fall into the very much narrower definition of 'building'. This also holds good for pieces of machinery which are housed in buildings that are in no way listable. [If the building is listed, the machinery may be protected by virtue of section 1(5) of the Planning (Listed Buildings & Conservation Areas) Act 1990 – see Chapter 5]. That said, in recent years the statutory lists have included items such as lock gates and even the odd village pump that are in something of a grey area, although they are 'structures or erections' in terms of the listing legislation.

Having defined a monument, we must next define an ancient monument. Here, we must turn to section 61(12) of the 1979 Act, which states that the definition embraces monuments which are in the opinion of the Secretary of State (for National Heritage) of public interest by reason of the historic, architectural, traditional, artistic or archaeological interest attached to them. Again, this is a much wider and looser definition than the 'special architectural or historic interest' that dictates whether a building should be listed or not.

This permissiveness goes even wider. For although we use the term 'ancient monument' and think of long barrows, Stonehenge, Hadrian's Wall and medieval castles, there is in fact no requirement for a monument to be ancient at all.There is no equivalent to the date-oriented criteria for listing; and although rarity value is important, as we shall see, there is nothing to stop comparatively modern structures being included in the definition. In fact, some Second World War defence works were scheduled long before the Secretary of State decided that such recent structures were eligible for listing.

Finally, we come to the definition of a scheduled ancient monument. Section 1 of the 1979 Act defines the schedule, which is maintained for the purposes of the Act. It includes all ancient monuments scheduled under earlier legislation – the 1913 and 1931 Acts – and also any ancient monument which the Secretary of State, having consulted the Commission, considers to be of national importance.

Not surprisingly, the definition of a scheduled ancient monument overlaps with that for a listed building, and many structures are both scheduled and listed. However, there are two main types of structure that cannot be scheduled, because they are excluded from the definition of a monument:

1. an ecclesiastical building which is used for ecclesiastical purposes (these can of course be listed);
2. a wreck, including the site of a wreck, protected by an order under the Protection of Wrecks Act 1973.

Further, a structure which is used as a dwelling-house (a curious legal phrase, for what other type of house is there?) cannot be scheduled – although it can be a monument – unless it is simply inhabited by a caretaker.

Given the very wide definition of a scheduled ancient monument, we might expect there to be lots of them. But not a bit of it. There are in fact about 15 000 of them. The clue here is the definition of national importance.The term is interpreted very strictly both by the Secretary of State and by the Commission, and the number of additions to the schedule has in recent years been fairly small.

Despite the use of the misnomer 'ancient', there is a heavy bias towards the prehistoric. In February 1984, it was estimated that of the total ancient monuments

61% were prehistoric
8% were Roman
3% were early medieval (5th century–1066)
21% were medieval (1066–1540)
7% were post-medieval.

Everyone concerned, however, acknowledges that the number of ancient monuments that have been scheduled is very low. Because of their nature and location, some monuments are in danger of disappearing altogether – if not from gentle decay then because they may be ploughed under. In other cases, the increasingly sophisticated technology and methodology used in modern archaeological research is revealing monuments where no monuments were thought to be. These trends and the need to obtain a balanced comprehensive sample have encouraged English Heritage to embark on a new Monuments Protection Programme which it is expected will raise the numbers of scheduled ancient monuments to around 30 000 by 2003.

8.2
How monuments are chosen

The criteria for selecting ancient monuments for scheduling are a lot more generally expressed than those for listing buildings. As with listing, the criteria are non-statutory. The Secretary of State has said that he will take the following points into account.

1. *Survival and condition* In other words, how much of the original fabric remains, and what condition it is in.
2. *Period* The age of the monument and whether it characterizes a period.
3. *Rarity* The selection is meant to include the typical and commonplace as well as the rare, but a premium is put on items that are so scarce that all those retaining any archaeological potential should be preserved. One interesting departure from listing practice in this respect is that the Secretary of State will take into account the distribution of the type of monument regionally as well as nationally.
4. *Fragility and vulnerability* This particularly applies to field monuments that may be destroyed by a single ploughing, or standing structures the value of which may be compromised and reduced by neglect. For these particularly vulnerable monuments, scheduling can provide an extra degree of protection – even where, for instance, they may already be listed.
5. *Diversity* Some monuments may have a number of factors pointing to their being scheduled, even though they may be lacking a single important attribute.

6. *Documentation* Records – both those contemporary with the monument's construction and those relating to earlier archaeological investigation – may point up its significance.
7. *Group value* The criterion here is similar to that for the group value of listed buildings. Simply, the value of an individual monument may be enhanced by its association with a number of other related monuments.
8. *Potential* Sometimes, an ancient monument may be scheduled where it can be reasonably anticipated that the evidence for its significance exists even though it is not yet clear. This is particularly the case with sites where thorough excavation may not yet have been carried out.

As in the case of listing, the criteria leave open considerable room for subjective assessment – perhaps even more so, in some cases, given the lack of documentary or other evidence to support the view of the expert eye.

8.3
The mechanics of scheduling

The mechanics of scheduling are not unlike those for listing. Most are carried out as part of the Monuments Protection Programme, but anyone may put forward a candidate for scheduling, and requests of this sort should be addressed to the Department of National Heritage. It is helpful if the request is accompanied by plans, photographs and any known details of the site. This information will then be sent to the Commission where an inspector will look at it and if necessary carry out a site visit. He will judge the monument by the standards set out in the previous section, and the judgment will be tough. If he thinks the site is good enough for scheduling, the owner will usually be notified and the inspector will forward a recommendation to the Ancient Monuments Advisory Committee of the Commission for endorsement; and the Commission's recommendation will go to the Department for decision. The owner is then notified of the outcome. If the decision is to schedule, the Commission will send the owner and the local planning authority for the area a copy of the schedule, and the latter will register this as a land charge. The main difference between the mechanics of listing and scheduling is that the Secretary of State's power to schedule is purely discretionary. There is not the statutory duty that exists in the case of listing.

8.4
Acquisition and guardianship

The Secretary of State has the power to acquire an ancient monument. This can take place in one of three ways: by agreement; by a gift; or by compulsory acquisition. Understandably, the Secretary of State is usually reluctant to take the last course, and this will only be pursued after consultation with the Commission and only then if it is absolutely necessary to secure the preservation of the monument.

The more common way of helping to preserve an ancient monument is to take it into guardianship. Most owners are obviously enough not expert in the preservation of historic structures or features, and guardianship ensures that while they remain as owners the responsibility for care, maintenance and management is vested in the Secretary of State, the Commission or a local authority. Guardianship arrangements are entirely voluntary, and from the owner's point of view the only drawback is the obligation to permit public access to the monument. Guardianship is a well-established feature of the ancient monuments legislation. It has been with us since the 1913 Act and there are now over 400 monuments in the guardianship of the Commission alone.

8.5
Repairs

Unless a scheduled ancient monument is in guardianship, the responsibility for keeping it properly maintained and repaired rests with the owner. The position here is like that relating to listed buildings. And, as with listed buildings, there is a power available to the Secretary of State to carry out works himself where they are necessary for the preservation of the monument. The power, which exists through section 5 of the 1979 Act, also allows the Secretary of State to authorize the Commission to carry out the works. The owner and/or occupier has to be given seven days notice of the intention to carry out the work – again akin to the listed building position. But the procedure then departs in not allowing the Secretary of State or the Commission to recoup the costs they have incurred from the owner. Not surprisingly, the power is used very sparingly.

More commonly, the Commission or the local authority may be able to offer grants to help preserve the monument. That does not mean that grant is easy to obtain, as we shall see in Chapter 9. But it does help out in a situation where the usual reliance on an owner's good economic sense to look after his/her property may not hold good. For unlike a listed building, an ancient monument will probably not be the owner's house or factory or workshop. It is unlikely to add anything to the value of his/her property. In fact, the ancient monument may actually be a blessed nuisance, especially if it obstructs the ploughing of a field or the redevelopment of a site. In those circumstances, even a small grant can be a useful carrot to complement the stick of urgent repair work being carried out by the Commission or the Secretary of State.

8.6
Descheduling

The Secretary of State has a power to amend the schedule at any time, as with the statutory lists. Usually, this occurs only where the monument has physically ceased to exist, its fragility having finally given way; or where new evidence shows that it does not in fact possess the national importance that it was thought to have; or where its preservation is simply not practicable because of the money or resources involved. To this, we must add those unfortunate cases – luckily still rare – where a monument is destroyed without the necessary consent.

As with listing, there is no formal right of appeal against descheduling, and although the Secretary of State's power is discretionary, his decision is final. But there is nothing to stop an owner from making representations that the monument does not possess the national interest ascribed to it. If the Secretary of State accepts the case (having consulted the Commission), then he will remove the monument from the schedule. If his representations do not succeed, then his only course is to apply for scheduled monument consent for the monument's removal.

It has to be said that very few monuments are descheduled. In the past, the figure has been about a dozen a year. Scheduling provides a pretty sound form of protection, and owners are, in the vast majority of cases, willing to act responsibly to help secure their monument's future.

8.7
Scheduled monument consent

As with listed buildings, the fact that monument is scheduled does not mean that it will necessarily be preserved intact for all time; but it does ensure that there is a control mechanism that examines the case for its preservation separately from the case for redeveloping the site. This mechanism is the scheduled monument consent (SMC) procedure. In many ways, it mirrors that for listed building consent, but there are three main important points where the systems differ.

1. Applications for SMC are always made to the Secretary of State for National Heritage rather than to the local planning authority; and this means that there is consequently no right of appeal (although remedy through judicial review may be possible if the administration of the application has been unfair to one of the parties).
2. Applicants for SMC are given the *provisional* views of the Secretary of State before the final decision is taken, and may make their views known to the Secretary of State (this is an administrative arrangement rather than a legal requirement).
3. The SMC procedure is a matter between the applicant, the owner of the land if different and the Secretary of State (and the Commission, who advise the Secretary of State) There is no requirement to advertise applications for SMC, which might invite third party representations; nor indeed is there any requirement to involve the local planning authority, despite the fact that they may be considering a planning application running in parallel.

The general requirement to obtain scheduled monument consent is contained in section 2 of the 1979 Act. This makes clear that anyone who wishes to do

- any works which would result in the monument's destruction or demolition, or which would cause any damage to it; or

- any work for the purposes of removing or repairing the monument or any part of it; or
- any work altering or adding to the monument; or
- any flooding or tipping operations on land in, on or under which there is a scheduled ancient monument,

requires the consent of the Secretary of State in writing.

There are some exceptions to this rule. Just as the Permitted Development Order grants a general planning permission for certain specified works, so the Ancient Monuments (Class Consents) Order 1981 which is made under section 3 of the 1979 Act, grants a general scheduled monument consent for five classes of development. These are:

1. agricultural, horticultural or forestry work of a kind that was carried out on the site for the five years preceding 1981, provided that it does not in general disturb the soil below the maximum depth affected by normal ploughing;
2. work carried out more than 10 metres below ground level by the National Coal Board and its licensees;
3. minor repair and maintenance work carried out by the British Waterways Board and any work required by them to help keep a canal functioning;
4. work for the repair or maintenance of machinery, so long as it does not involve a material alteration to the monument;
5. work essential for the purposes of health and safety.

To this list, the Ancient Monuments (Class Consents) (Amendment) Order 1984 added:

6. work carried out by the Commission.

Four further minor clauses of development were added by a further amendment order in 1994.

The only defences that are available to the claim that an offence has been committed are those relating to due diligence (i.e. that all reasonable precautions were taken to avoid the destruction or demolition of a monument or to adhere to the conditions imposed in a consent; or that in some cases of a concealed monument that its existence was simply not known to the defendant) or the 'urgently necessary in the interests of health and safety' defence that we encountered in the case of listed building offences. In general, the defences available are considerably more generous than those allowed in the case of breaches of listed building control. There, breaches constitute offences of strict liability, and the amendments to the health and safety provision imposed by the Housing & Planning Act 1986 have made that one defence a lot more difficult to use than the one available in the case of ancient monuments. This seems fair enough. Listed buildings are there for all to see. It is pretty hard to demolish or alter one unknowingly. But many ancient monuments are under fields, and their extent and nature are sometimes not known: hence the 'due diligence' defence presumably. The Courts have supported this interpretation. In the cases of *R* v. *J.O. Sims Ltd* (1992) and *R* v. *Simpson (1993)* the Court of Appeal mitigated penalties imposed by the Crown Court because the defendants had not set out to destroy the monuments concerned.

Failure to obtain scheduled monument consent, or to comply with a condition attached to a consent, is an offence. The penalty will be a fine up to a statutory maximum in the Magistrates' Court (the limit is uprated from time to time in line with inflation); or an unlimited amount on conviction on indictment (i.e. at the Crown Court). Where a protected monument is damaged or destroyed there can not only be a fine, but also the prospect of imprisonment.

Applications for scheduled monument consent must be addressed to the Secretary of State for National Heritage (at 2–4 Cockspur Street, London SW1Y 5DH): he will seek the advice of professional advisers in the Commission, but the decision, as with scheduling, rests with the Secretary of State.

Applications for SMC are made under section 2(11) of the 1979 Act. The Ancient Monuments (Applications for Scheduled Monument Consent) Regulations 1981 prescribe an application form and require that plans and drawings should accompany it. The Secretary of State is also empowered to ask for such other further information as thought necessary to deal with the application. There is also provision for the applicant to provide a certificate, like the one accompanying planning applications, stating that the applicant is either the owner of the land to which the application relates; or that the owner has been notified of the application; or that the applicant has truly been unable to trace the owner.

When the Secretary of State has reached a provisional view on the application, the applicant will normally be told. It will indicate whether the Secretary of State is disposed to grant consent, to grant it with conditions or to refuse it. The opportunity of a hearing must be offered to the applicant and any other person or body to whom it appears to the Secretary of State to be expedient. The Secretary of State is bound to consider the report of the inspector on the hearing, together with any representations made to the Secretary. But in fact this provision is comparatively rarely used.

Once granted, a scheduled monument consent lasts for five years unless there is a condition in it varying this period in any way. Consents must therefore be exercised within the prescribed timescale if they are to be of any use. The five year period here parallels that normally available for planning permissions and listed building consents.

The Secretary of State is also able to revoke or modify a consent subsequent to granting it. Consultation with the Commission is required in such cases, but the procedure in other respects is similar to that for revoking or modifying a planning permission. The power is useful in cases where a monument proves on investigation to be of greater importance than was first thought. But again, the power is one to be used in only a tiny minority of cases.

In certain rather unusual circumstances, it is possible to claim compensation for the refusal of scheduled monument consent or for its grant only with conditions. These are set out in section 7 of the 1979 Act. In short, compensation is only payable where a planning permission that was granted before the monument was scheduled has been frustrated; or where the refusal of consent relates to work which does not amount to development for planning purposes, or for which the Permitted Development Order would have granted permission; or where the consent would have enabled works to be carried out which were reasonably necessary for the continuation of any use of the monument for any purpose for which it was in use immediately before the date of the application for SMC. It is only fair to add that section 8 of the 1979 Act actually provides for the repayment of compensation where a consent is subsequently granted or modified in such a way that the frustration which led to the compensation has been removed. So beware!

8.8
Areas of archaeological importance

So far, we have dealt with Part I of the 1979 Act. Part II was brought into effect on 14 April 1982 and for the first time made specific provision for the particular problems associated with archaeology.

Up to that time, the only controls available were conditions attached to planning permissions or consents permitting access to the site during the course of work there to carry out archaeological investigations. The problem with this approach is that it required a fair degree of guesswork about the extent and nature of the archaeology that might be uncovered. Very often, the extent of the archaeological interest only becomes apparent in the course of building operations, as several well-publicized cases have demonstrated in recent years. On top of this, the condition-based approach did not always provide for adequate notice to be given to those bodies who might wish to conduct the archaeological investigations – university departments and the like – since there was no guarantee that work on site would commence as soon as the permission or consent had been granted.

Part II of the 1979 Act provides for a new method of tackling these problems. It allows for the designation of 'areas of archaeological importance'. Within these areas, an opportunity must be provided for archaeological examination and recording before development takes place and the evidence is obliterated. The evidence to date seems to be that, while the present system is not perfect, it is a great deal better than the approach that existed before 1982.

The basis of the present system lies in section 33 of the 1979 Act, which permits the Secretary of State to designate areas of archaeological importance: local planning authorities can also submit a designation order to the Secretary of State for confirmation. There is no right of appeal against inclusion in an order, although there will normally be a full round of consultation with all the parties concerned before it is made (consultation with English Heritage is mandatory), and the Secretary of State has the power to revoke the order or to reduce the size of the area to which it applies. Finally, the designation must be registered as a land charge.

Where an area has been designated, the developer is committing an offence if he or she carries out any work, or permits such work to be carried out, without first serving an operations notice on the local planning authority and then allowing six weeks to elapse thereafter. If the local authority is itself the developer, it must serve the notice on the Secretary of State. The operations notice should specify what exactly the proposed works are, the estimated start-date and the fact that anyone with an interest in the land has consented to the work being carried out.

The ball is then in the court of the 'investigating authority'. This slightly sinister-sounding term refers to those whom the Secretary of State has appointed to carry out any excavations. They will most often come from the archaeological department of a university or be an arm of the local authority itself. The investigating authority may excavate the site if within four weeks of the service of the operations notice they serve their own notice stating their intention to do so. They then have a period of four months and two weeks starting from the end of the six-week period required for the service of the operations notice. A little elementary mathematics shows that the developer must therefore do nothing for a period of up to six months – i.e. six weeks for the service and expiry of the operations notice plus (if the investigating authority want it) a further four months and two weeks for the excavations to take place. No development (provided that it has the necessary planning permission) can therefore be delayed by statute beyond six months to permit excavations to take place. This sometimes means there is a race against time to get the site investigated before the new development starts. In many instances, a cooperative developer will be happy to work in concert with the investigating authority and even to extend voluntarily the period available for excavation. But sometimes this is not possible. Money is tied up in the site and contractors may have been engaged to get on with the work. The six month limit is a compromise between the needs of archaeology and the interests of the developer. Occasionally, the compromise is not a happy one. There is a code of practice agreed by the British Archaeologists and Developers Liaison Group; but its provisions are purely voluntary. Sometimes, an operations notice is served in respect of work which will be carried out once site clearance is complete. In these circumstances, the developer has to notify the investigating authority as soon as the clearance work has been completed.

As with the requirement for scheduled monument consent, the Secretary of State has made an order which exempts certain types of operation from the requirements of section 35. The Areas of Archaeological Importance (Notification of Operations) (Exemption) Order 1984 spells out these exceptions. They include certain agricultural, forestry, tunnelling and mining operations, together with work in connection with the repair and maintenance of highways, waterways and main services – and the installation of the last-named.

There is another analogy with the scheduled monument consent position in respect of the defences that may be offered against any prosecution for breach of section 35. Once again, the 'due diligence' defence may be advanced (and for much the same reasons, since the very need for excavations suggests that both the developer and the archaeologist may be in some doubt about the precise value and extent of the site's interest); and again there is an 'interests of health and safety' provision. These defences are to be found in section 37 of the Act.

The problem with section 35 is that it does require a degree of foresight by the Secretary of State and local planning authorities. There must be at least some real prospect of excavation producing results before an area of archaeological importance is designated; indeed, it is only fair that this should be so, as the cavalier designation of such areas on suspicions and hunches could be very damaging to the developer's interests and in some cases might well serve no useful archaeological purpose at all. The problem is that there is no archaeological equivalent of spot-listing. Once operations are under way, there seems no way in which they can be halted if an interesting archaeological discovery is made – unless of course the developer is willing voluntarily to do so.

To encourage the spirit of cooperation, new advice was issued in 1990 in Planning Policy Guidance Note 16 (PPG16) *Archaeology & Planning*. This stressed the importance of early assessment of a site's archaeological significance involving the local planning authority, the developer and archaeological experts. It went on to put the onus on the developer to commission a field evaluation of the site, and generally at his or her expense. The PPG has had two important effects. First, it has made clear that the presence of archaeological remains are a material consideration in the planning process, and should be reflected in development plans. Second, it has encouraged a consistency of approach to archaeology and planning that was lacking in the absence of central guidance before. Its effects so far have been encouraging.

Archaeology is an expensive business, and considerable resources are devoted to this type of rescue archaeology as it is often called. In 1993/94, English Heritage spent £36 million in archaeology grants, and they are also undertaking a Monuments at Risk Study (MARS) which aims, by 1997, to assess the condition of archaeological remains nationwide. In addition, some of the funds spent by the

Royal Commission on Historical Monuments went on recording work at excavation sites.

8.9
Metal detectors

One useful addition that the 1979 Act made to the protection of ancient monuments and archaeological remains was contained in section 42. This controls the use of metal detectors in what is termed a 'protected place', which is defined as:

1. the site of a scheduled ancient monument;
2. any monument in the ownership or guardianship of the Secretary of State; or
3. an area of archaeological importance.

Section 42 provides that metal detectors shall not be used in a protected place without the written consent of the commission, and makes it a further offence to remove any object of archaeological or historical interest. The only defence to a charge of using a metal detector without written consent is to prove that it was being used for some other purpose than the location of antiquities. This seems on the face of it rather a tall order!

We should just mention here, if only because it is convenient, the matter of treasure trove. Strictly speaking, treasure trove applies to objects of pure gold or silver which were originally hidden by their owner. The finder is entitled to the full market value of the objects but they themselves go to the Crown. Some have called for a wider definition of treasure trove to prevent archaelogically interesting artefacts being bought and sold on the open market. In 1988, the Department of the Environment issued a consultation paper on 'portable antiquities' as it termed them; but no fresh legislation has emerged changing the existing arrangements.

8.10
Crown land

The provisions for dealing with Crown land under the 1979 Act are similar to those for listed buildings. The Department of the Environment will be notified of any development or work touching on a scheduled ancient monument or an area of archaeological importance. Normally, the Department will seek the views of the Commission on the proposals put to them.

8.11
Listing and scheduling

Finally, we must append a footnote about the position of those structures which are both listed and scheduled. The law is quite clear about which set of controls has precedence. Section 61 of the 1990 Act provides that listed building controls do not apply to scheduled ancient monuments, so that any works affecting them are subject only to scheduled monument consent.

Chapter 9

ENHANCING THE HERITAGE

So much for controls. We have considered up to now the framework of legislation that protects the heritage from proposals that threaten it. We must now turn to the means by which the heritage is enhanced.

In true British fashion, these comprise a mixture of carrot and stick. With more than 450000 listed buildings, and with some 15000 scheduled ancient monuments and over 8000 conservation areas – in England alone – the problem is too big for one agency to tackle alone. What has emerged over the years, therefore, is a variety of initiatives both statutory and non-statutory and embracing the efforts of central and local Government, voluntary agencies and the efforts of private individuals and companies. Legal sanctions and assistance have been assisted by a strong dose of good old-fashioned common sense. We will look in turn at the different ways in which action to enhance the heritage can be taken but always remembering that often different means can be combined to achieve the right results.

9.1
Repairs notices

We start with the stick. In general, there is no obligation on listed building owners to keep their properties in a state of good repair. Most will do so as a matter of good stewardship, and many more will do more than is strictly necessary because of the pride they feel in ownership. There can be problems where owners wish to carry out repairs or alterations which may not suit a building of special architectural or historic interest – the use of unsuitable paints or the installation of uPVC windows are among the most common such cases – but these can normally be sorted out by a sensible local authority officer with the British genius for compromise, or in the more extreme cases may be brought within the control system by virtue of being material alterations to the listed building. Much more serious is the case of the owner who neglects his/her listed building such that it falls into serious disrepair.

There are normally two possible reasons for this. The first is that the neglect is a deliberate act by an owner who wishes to demolish the building either because it is an economic burden or because he has in mind a more lucrative redevelopment of the site. There are in fact remarkably few such cases. They tend to occur in urban areas where land values are high or where the owner thinks there is a reasonable chance of obtaining planning permission for redevelopment. The second possible reason is that the owner does not have the means or the interest to keep the property in good repair and effectively has no option but to let it become neglected. The obvious example is the country house (particularly one where the twin enemies of wet or dry rot and the deathwatch beetle have made their mark): such properties are almost prohibitively expensive to maintain at the best of times. But other less dramatic cases can also come into this category: people living on fixed incomes or pensions in even the most modest properties can find the costs of maintenance beyond them; an industrialist or a farmer, especially if pressed for cash, will concentrate expenditure on those portions of the property which are in everyday use and may neglect out-buildings even though they may be listed or fall within curtilage controls.

It is easy enough to raise a hullabaloo about the owners who neglect their listed property. Local planning authorities are frequently criticized for not using the powers available to them either often enough or quickly enough. but as the examples quoted above show, right is not always wholly on the side of conservation. Some would argue, and do, that an owner who is unable to maintain a listed property should be forced to sell it. The law does indeed allow for this as we shall see. But it is a nice philosophical and indeed political point whether owners should have their properties taken away because the state has decided that they are of special interest and should be maintained according to certain standards. Owners in such circumstances can feel understandably aggrieved that they have been expropriated like some Russian kulak. On the other hand, if the property is of acknowledged national interest and its owner is unable or unwilling to keep it in good repair, there is an argument for bringing it into public ownership so that the public can pay the price of its maintenance (or, more commonly, hand it on to someone who can). The use of repairs notices, let alone compulsory acquisition, is almost always a difficult area where planning authorities understandably proceed with considerable caution.

Where a listed building is in a state of disrepair, local authorities have three possible courses of action. In fact, before adopting any of them, the authority will probably try to enter a dialogue with the owner to see if a way of rectifying the situation is possible without resorting to legal action. Such action is usually something of a last resort, although the knowledge that it is available is a powerful weapon in the authority's hands.

The first course is available only if the properties concerned are houses or dwellings. This is the use of the powers contained in sections 189–90 of the Housing Act 1985. These are powers applicable to all houses or dwellings whether listed or not, and are relevant where the properties are considered to be unfit or in need of substantial repairs which can be carried out at reasonable expense. In addition, in housing action areas and general improvement areas, authorities are able under Parts VII and VIII of the Act to serve improvement notices on the owners of dwellings which do not have standard amenities and which are considered to be capable of improvement at reasonable expense.

But listing is less concerned with the delights of inside toilets and bathrooms than with the future of the fabric of the building itself. And of course many listed buildings do not fall within the ambit of the Housing Acts. The second possible course of action is the most generally applicable, not least because it is the only one that covers all types of listed buildings. This is the power available to local authorities (and in London to English Heritage as well) under sections 47–48 of the 1990 Act to serve a repairs notice on the owner of a listed building where 'reasonable steps are not being taken for properly preserving it'. The notice must be served on the owner and should specify the works which the authority consider reasonably necessary for the proper preservation of the building and the effect of the provisions of the Act. The works must refer to the preservation of the building as it was when listed (which might be some time ago) rather than as it was at the time the notice was served. If at the end of two months those reasonable steps have not been taken, the authority can, with the consent of the Secretary of State, acquire the building compulsorily.

And ay, there's the rub. For unless the authority are determined to pursue the matter to compulsory acquisition if necessary, then the repairs notice is, in the immortal words of the youthful Daisy Ashford, so much 'piffle before the wind'. It is this aspect of the repairs notice provisions of sections 47–48 that deters so many planning authorities from using them. And understandably so, and even rightly so. For what Parliament seems to have been saying in making this provision is that local authorities should put their money where their mouth is: the repairs notice procedure is not one lightly to be adopted.

For this reason, and to avoid a game of bluff and double bluff with the listed building owner, many authorities try to line up a prospective purchaser before the repairs notice is served, both to be sure that they are not landed with a property that they do not want (and possibly cannot afford) and to demonstrate to the owner that there is an alternative freeholder in the wings. Finding such an alternative can be a tricky mater. The condition and location of the building and its possible capacity for modification to a new use will all be critical factors. The national amenity societies may be able to indicate a possible purchaser, and so might the Buildings at Risk Officer of English Heritage. It may be that by putting the prospective purchaser in touch with the owner, a sale can be carried through without the need for repairs and compulsory purchase notices.

Finally, we should record that it is open to the Secretary of State to take action under sections 47–48. It is unlikely that this would be done unless there was a very strong case of national importance, and the local authority concerned was unwilling to take action.

The third form of repairs notice is that which can be served under section 54 of the 1990 Act. This section applies to urgent repairs which are necessary to secure the preservation of unoccupied listed buildings (or in the case of occupied buildings, those parts which are not in use). The Secretary of State under section 76 may also direct that the section should apply to a building in a conservation area where it is considered that the preservation of the building is important for maintaining the character or appearance of the area. Again, both the Secretary of State and local planning authorities (and in London, English Heritage) have concurrent powers to serve section 54 notices, although again the Secretary of State is unlikely to use this power except in the most extreme circumstances: should he choose to do so, English Heritage may be authorized to carry out the work on the Secretary of State's behalf.

There are two important points we must make in connection with section 54 notices. First, they are for use only in respect of *urgent* repairs. This means that they cover only emergency repairs – that is, the minimum necessary to keep a building wind and weatherproof and safe against vandals. It really is tarpaulin over the roof stuff, together with the use of temporary scaffolding and props where there is a danger of collapse. The guiding principle is that the work done to a building under section 54 should be 'the minimum required for its preservation and be carried out at a reasonable cost'.

This brings us neatly to the second point, which is that under section 55, the Secretary of State, the planning authority or English Heritage is able to recover from the owner the cost of the repairs that are carried out. This includes any continuing expenses involved in making available the apparatus or material used. This really does sound draconian, although the power has been used sparingly in practice. The owner has 28 days from the service of the notice to make representations to the Secretary of State against payment. There are three grounds for doing so:

1. that some of all the works were unnecessary for the preservation of the building: this guards against local authorities giving too generous an interpretation to urgent repairs (and perhaps going beyond what the Act intends);
2. in the case of work designed to give temporary support or shelter that the temporary arrangements have continued for an unreasonable period: a curious ground, since there is no obvious way in which the temporary works could be made permanent without the cooperation of the owner (the authority could of course follow up their urgent repairs with action under sections 47–48, but this would take an absolute minimum of two months);
3. that the amount specified in the notice is unreasonable or that its recovery would cause the owner hardship.

It is probably the third sub-head here which has deterred authorities from making too much use of section 54, for even the most elementary and crude repairs are likely to prove costly and beyond the means of many owners. But the very fact that costs can be recovered at all is a powerful weapon in the planning authority's armoury, and the seven days' notice that is all that is required between service and the works being carried out must concentrate the minds of some owners wonderfully on the question of maintaining their properties.

9.2
Grants and loans

It is sometime argued by owners of listed buildings that since central Government have designated their properties as being of special architectural or historic interest they should be prepared to make a contribution towards their upkeep. As we have explained, the fact that a building has been listed places no special obligations on the owner other than the extreme cases where the proper preservation of the building itself may be threatened and the use of a repairs notice becomes necessary. It is true that an owner may be required to use more expensive specialist materials and craftsmen in the course of carrying out alterations (these may indeed be conditions of the grant of consent), but there are no special obligations placed on him/her as regards the upkeep of his/her property: old buildings are old buildings and often require more expense and more expertise than new ones – that is a fact of life and has nothing to do with whether they are listed or not. Nevertheless, we can identify up to six possible sources of grant which listed building owners *may* be eligible to receive. These are in addition to the normal range of grants available to owners of listed and unlisted buildings – for instance, those available for substandard housing from local authorities.

9.2.1 Historic Building and Ancient Monuments Act grants

There are a number of grants available under this Act. The ones of main interest to most owners are those payable under section 3A, which can be used for:

1. the repair or maintenance of buildings in England of outstanding historic interest (in practice this means Grade I and Grade II* buildings, although buildings originally graded at II sometimes are considered eligible where they are thought on a reassessment to be worth a higher grading);
2. the upkeep of land adjacent to such a building;

3. the repair or maintenance of objects kept in such buildings;
4. the upkeep of gardens or land of outstanding architectural or historic interest.

Other sections allow for the provision of grants to local authorities towards the costs of compulsory acquisition under section 47; and for the provision of grant to the National Trust for the provision of land, buildings and gardens of outstanding interest.

Section 3A grants are administered solely by the Commission without reference to the Secretary of State (although he provides the funds for them). Applications should thus be addressed to the Commission.

9.2.2 Conservation area grants

These are made under section 77 of the 1990 Act, and are paid where the work to be undertaken will make a significant contribution towards preserving or enhancing the character or appearance of a conservation area. Originally, these grants were payable only for work in outstanding conservation areas, but now all conservation areas are eligible. Grants are given by the Commission, but applications are normally channelled or supported through local planning authorities.

9.2.3 Town scheme grants

These are paid under section 80 of the 1990 Act and are again administered by the Commission. Grants are paid in respect of expenditure on the repair of a building which is in a town scheme and appears to be of architectural or historic interest. Town schemes are run jointly by the commission and the local authority and are directed at enhancing the appearance of a historic conservation area. They are usually more comprehensive in scope than the type of scheme for which a section 77 grant would be available and are concerned with conserving the fabric of buildings as well as their appearance.

9.2.4 Conservation area partnerships

English Heritage are now refocusing the grant-aid they give for buildings in conservation areas. They are seeking to establish Conservation Area Partnerships (CAPs) with selected local authorities to concentrate joint resources on the areas of greatest need. Fifteen pilot projects were established in 1994 and it is expected that by 1997 CAPs will be, in all but a few cases, the single formal means of directing English Heritage funding into conservation areas.

9.2.5 Local authority grants

Local authorities have their own discretionary power under section 57 of the 1990 Act to make grants or loans towards the repair or maintenance of buildings of architectural or historic interest (whether listed, i.e. of special interest, or not). Funds are usually very limited, but some authorities make considerable use of this power.

9.2.6 London-only grant

Following the abolition of the Greater London Council, English Heritage obtained a power under the Local Government Act 1985 to make grants for the repair of any building within the Greater London area which appeared to be of architectural or historic interest (again, whether or not it is listed).

9.2.7 European Union grants

Since 1984, the European Union has offered grants towards the preservation of Europe's architectural heritage. A different theme is set each year and applications are invited through an advertisement in the *Journal of The European Communities*. Applications are normally vetted by English Heritage.

9.2.8 National Heritage Memorial Fund and the National Lottery

The Fund was established in 1980 as the successor to the National Land Fund. It is able to make grants and loans *inter alia* towards the acquisition, maintenance or preservation of any land, building or structure which is of outstanding scenic, historic, aesthetic, architectural or scientific interest. Applications should be made to the Trustees.

The NHMF will also be the vehicle for distributing funds from the National Lottery to heritage projects. It is anticipated that these will amount to some £320 million annually when lottery income peaks. Historic buildings will be only one of the heritage areas eligible for funds and at present limitations on NHMF's powers make it impossible for private individuals or profit-distributing companies to benefit. But, lottery funds will be in addition to current Government expenditure and promise to be a valuable new source of income.

9.2.9 **Ancient monuments**

In the case of ancient monuments, section 24 of the Ancient Monuments & Archaeological Areas Act 1979 allows for grants towards the acquisition, re-siting, preservation, maintenance or management of an ancient monument. Section 45 also provides for assistance towards the cost of any archaeological investigations on any land. The Commission are responsible for such grants.

Where it is not possible to obtain grant, or grant sufficient to cover all the costs of repair or restoration, it may be possible to obtain a loan. These may be available from conventional sources of finance, although the commercial banks are not known for their sense of adventure when it comes to taking risks. In some cases it may be possible to obtain a loan from a local building preservation trust. The growth of such institutions in the last 15 years has been a very heartening development, and many of them have achieved inspiring results. They provide loan capital on a revolving fund basis – that is to say, loans are made from the income that comes from the repayment of past loans. Since they are not in business to produce a profit and are run on a shoestring, their overheads are minimal. The local trusts themselves may receive loan capital from the Architectural Heritage Fund, which we mentioned in Chapter 4, and which was one of the most successful legacies of European Architectural Heritage Year in 1975.

Loans certainly look a less attractive prospect to most people than do grants. But it is worth remembering that most grants are normally paid in arrears, so that a loan may be necessary to fund the work in the first place anyway. Anyone contemplating a grant should also remember that it will probably be accompanied by a set of stringent conditions specifying such things as the materials to be used, the method of working and in some cases even the specialist contractors that may be employed. There will also be provision for the early repayment of the grant, or of a proportion of it, if the property is re-sold within a specified period of years from when the work is carried out: this is designed to discourage simple profiteering (although it could be argued in today's mobile society that it discourages many ordinary owners who may in the course of their careers have to move every two or three years). The balance of argument between grants and loans is narrower than it first appears, and the best advice is to shop around and see what is available. Again, the conservation officer of the local planning authority can often provide some helpful leads.

Even where grant is given, it is unlikely to cover more than a proportion of the costs. The means of the owner and the ground rules for the award of grant will also be relevant factors. In looking at the grant application, someone is bound to ask if the work would be carried out anyway: and whether, if it is, and grant were awarded towards the cost, it would act as a catalyst for further action in the area by the owners of other historic buildings. There are no hard and fast rules to cover all grant applications, but in general we can say:

- if the building is listed Grade I or II*, it stands a reasonable chance of obtaining a repair grant;
- if the building is sited in a town scheme and is of architectural or historic interest (it does not *have* to be listed), it has the possibility of repair grant, especially if it is prominent or its restoration would be a catalyst for further action in the vicinity;
- if the building is prominently sited in a conservation area, it may be eligible to receive conservation area grant towards the restoration of its facade(s) or roof;
- if the building is a dwelling but is substandard as accommodation, it may be possible to obtain grants under the Housing Acts;
- if a new use is being found for an old building, and the building is of local or national interest, then there is the possibility of a loan through a revolving fund if one exists in the area, or conceivably from the Architectural Heritage Fund;
- if the building is situated in London, there is the possibility of help from the Commission, although funds are, as elsewhere, very limited;
- there is everywhere the possibility of grant or loan from local authorities themselves using their powers under the 1990 Act; but again, funds are very limited and the pressures great.

Separate funds are available for churches, and an approach to the local Diocesan Advisory Council may prove worthwhile. Over 250 redundant Anglican churches, for instance, are vested in the Redundant Churches Fund, which is grant-aided by the Government and the Church Commissioners. There is also currently a separate Cathedral Repair Grants scheme managed by English Heritage.

Between 1984/85 and 1993/94, the grants handed out by English Heritage grew from £21.4 million to £41.7 million. These may not be large sums in the range of central and local government expenditure, but they do represent a very considerable boost to the conservation of our heritage. The purpose of most grant-aid is not after all that of a direct subsidy: rather it is a pump-primer to encourage similar sums to be forthcoming from other sources. Perhaps it would be fairer, although alas it is not possible, to add to the grant that is given those sums which were spent on conservation by private trusts, firms and individuals which might not otherwise have been spent without the incentive of the grant.

One final word for the grant-seeker. Most grant-awarding bodies are not averse to schemes qualifying for cocktails of different grant, such that each award can be a building brick towards achieving the total. This is particularly true of grants made under the Housing Acts. It is worth enquiring from the local authority or the Commission as the conditions under which grants are paid vary considerably.

9.3
Tax incentives

With the exception of Value Added Tax (VAT), there are no great tax incentives that can be enjoyed by the vast majority of owners of listed buildings. The only income tax relief available is that for which any property may be eligible if it is run as, or for, a business. There are no special concessions in respect of historic buildings or ancient monuments. The arguments here are the same as those that apply against the disbursement of large sums of grant by the state. The repair of their property is a reasonable expense that owners can be expected to undertake and is not particularly affected by the fact that the property is listed.

Some buildings may now qualify for Inheritance Tax Relief. Any building or ancient monument is in theory eligible, but in fact only those which are outstanding will qualify. Those in receipt of grant given under section 3A of the 1953 Act are considered to have a good case for being considered outstanding in the eyes of the Inland Revenue, but before taking a decision, their Capital Taxes Office will consult the Commission.

Relief is normally given on condition that agreed steps will be taken to secure reasonable public access and that the property will be properly maintained and preserved. Relief may also be obtained if the property is transferred to the Inland Revenue in satisfaction of Inheritance Tax, or if it is transferred to a UK charity or to a body concerned with the preservation of the national heritage or to some other approved non-profit-making body. Further details of the complex position here can be found from the leaflets 'Capital Taxation and the National Heritage' (IR67) and 'Inheritance Tax' (IHT1) available from local offices of the Inland Revenue. It is also as well to secure the services of a good tax accountant to seek a way through the maze of regulations and to negotiate with the Inland Revenue where necessary.

For the majority of listed building owners, the most valuable tax incentive is that available in respect of VAT. Repairs and alterations to unlisted buildings are subject to VAT at the normal rates. However, alterations (but not repairs) to listed buildings can be exempt from VAT. The liability rules here are complex following changes in the Finance Act 1989. These in turn were made necessary because the relief that used to exist for approved alterations to non-domestic protected buildings (the term used by Customs and Excise to denote ancient monuments and listed buildings) had to be withdrawn following a judgment in the European Court of Justice in June 1988.

Briefly, the position now is as follows.

1. *Contractor to client* (i.e. the usual arrangement where an owner obtains the professional services of a contractor to carry out work).

    VAT zero-rating is available for approved alterations to those protected buildings which:
    (a) are designed to remain as or become dwellings; or
    (b) are to be used solely for certain communal residential purposes or for non-business charity purposes (listed churches qualify under this heading).

    'Approved alterations' are works which require and obtain scheduled monument consent or listed building consent.

    All other work done by contractors is standard-rated – in other words, there is no relief for any work carried out to protected buildings not qualifying under (a) or (b) and no relief at all for repairs or for alterations which do not require consent.

2. *Sale or long lease by developer* (i.e. an owner carrying out his/her own work).

VAT zero-rating is available if the developer undertakes a substantial reconstruction of a protected building which qualifies under 1(a) or (b) above. 'Substantial reconstruction' here is defined in two ways:

(a) either the protected building has to be in effect gutted; or

(b) at least 60% of the works have to be such that they would have qualified for zero-rating if done by a contractor.

The most common complaint about these arrangements is that the Government does not grant relief on repairs to protected buildings. The argument here is that any property owner has to carry out repairs to property from time to time, irrespective of whether the building is protected or not: and that there is accordingly little argument for giving the owner of a listed building or an ancient monument preferential treatment. As it is the VAT concessions offer a very valuable incentive in one area where it is needed – namely, the alteration and conversion of protected buildings to new uses. Further information is given in a leaflet available from any local office of HM Customs and Excise entitled *Protected Buildings (Listed Buildings and Scheduled Monuments)* (leaflet number 708/1/85). The local office should also be able to help with individual questions and cases.

9.4
New uses for old buildings

But all the grants, loans and tax incentives in the world would not be enough by themselves to protect the heritage.That also takes a general will on the part of developers and planning authorities, and a recognition that such a course makes economic sense. The danger otherwise would be in a heritage slipping into a gentle decline.That still seemed possible 25 years ago. The legislative framework was in place, but there remained the problem of what to do with those buildings which had outlived their original use. Churches, factories and country houses posed particular problems. So too did less spectacular difficulties, such as the use of the upper floors of shops in historic areas, the neglect of which could endanger entire buildings.

There was of course nothing new about finding new uses for old buildings. It has been practiced since the earliest times. It was perhaps only the preoccupation with comprehensive redevelopment in the 1950s and 1960s that obscured this fact. In the new throwaway society, re-use seemed less attractive than constructing something glitteringly new, even where the glitter rapidly wore off. Once again, it was disillusionment with such a philosophy –the falling of scales from eyes that we chronicled in Chapter 1 – that brought the change of attitude. Most important was the change in attitude that was experienced by Government itself. The new Department of the Environment was well abreast, if not actually ahead, of the time when it produced a modest but well-illustrated booklet in 1971 entitled *New Life for Old Buildings*. The planners and the developers quickly got the message. It became easier in many instances to secure planning permission for the conversion of a building than for its demolition and the construction of a new building on the same site. This was particularly true of local landmark buildings in towns, such as churches, whose destruction could raise an outcry among local residents; and for a whole range of developments in the countryside where greenfield development was unlikely to be popular with the planners and which was often against the tenor of the new local plans.

The1970s and 1980s saw a snowballing of the trend towards new uses. The ingenuity of a generation of architects has been tested in achieving suitable conversions and the results in most instances have been impressive. The anti-modernist reaction has had its effect upon business and the public and there seems to be a clear preference for re-use over new build. Churches, which seemed to pose almost intractable problems on account of their size and lack of light, have been the subject of ingenious solutions [perhaps inspired in part by the DoE's second foray into this field with *New Life for Old Churches* (1978)]. Country houses, whose isolation from the rest of the community, absolutely and relatively, once seemed an insuperable bar to their acquiring a new use, are now frequently the subject of conversion to flats or hotel use with little loss of the original fabric or proportions. And the farmer who might once have left a barn to decay and collapse may not realize he has an asset to use if it can be converted and resold as a house, or turned into residential accommodation for hikers and school and college parties. Few of these conversions take place with the help of grant-aid. Many use revolving funds of the kind we have described: but the majority rely on the more orthodox sources of finance open to everyone. They can do so because they pay their way. The conversion of old buildings should not be a loss-making activity.

For those contemplating what use can be made of an old building, a feasibility study is essential. This should examine four basic questions.

1. The present use of the building: can it still be used for this with or without modification to the structure? This is likely to be the least risky course if at all feasible.
2. What is the structural condition of the building? Is it sound? If not, what are the weak points and how do these relate to any possible alternative uses?
3. What other uses might be suitable for the building? This is where the specialist knowledge of architects can be invaluable, not least because they know what has been done with similar structures elsewhere.
4. What funds are available, and how do these fit in with the possibilities explored in the rest of the study?

A specialist architect and surveyor are necessary to produce such a study, but some informal guidance should be available from the local authority's own conservation staff: and they should be able to nominate firms and individuals who might be able to take the work forward. The Buildings at Risk Officer at English Heritage should also be able to help if necessary.

The feasibility study should at least attempt some costings, as these will be needed in presenting it to likely sources of finance. The study will also need to be discussed with the local planning authority in order to assess the likelihood of obtaining the necessary consent for the alterations and any partial demolition that is necessary. Their attitude will almost certainly be positive. They are enjoined by the Secretary of State in PPG15 to find new uses wherever possible. Paragraph 3.10 asks them to be flexible in dealing with planning applications for changes of use of buildings of architectural or historic interest or other applications for consent for works associated with a change of use. Paragraph 2.18 bluntly asserts

New uses may often be the key to a building's or area's preservation, and controls over land use, density, plot ratio, daylighting and other planning matters should be exercised sympathetically where this would enable an historic building or area to be given a new lease of life.

Other paragraphs of the circular tackle the importance of preserving and protecting as much of the original fabric as possible. Large old houses, for instance, with high ceilings and grand staircases and lobbies can often be more suitable for office than residential use – although, as we have seen, sensitive conversions into flats have been achieved with some country houses.This is where the skill of the architect comes to the fore.

It is easy to deride the trend for re-use. A latter-day Osbert Lancaster could have great fun with some of the less sensitive barn conversions that have appeared up and down the country. And some of the best re-uses have been those which have left the original fabric substantially intact (we are now coming to recognize that some of our most fortunate cinemas were those converted into bingo halls: their new managers did not endlessly subdivide them into mini-cinemas in their efforts to retain their dwindling audiences). But without re-use many of our listed buildings would have gently faded away or been demolished to make way for a replacement more in tune with today's needs.There is a school of thought that says it is sad that so many chapels have become workshops; that old mill buildings should now house squash courts and craft centres; and that we have sacrificed the dignity of these buildings in our efforts to keep them in existence. But that is the argument of a minority. The majority view is that new use is better than no use at all, and that by making yesterday's architecture in tune with today's requirements we can prove its value to new generations and show them that the past is not something which can simply be seen in a museum or with the help of an English Heritage season ticket. The rapid changes that our society is witnessing might sweep all before it were we not prepared to modify what we already possess for future purposes. In the 1970s, it was said that small was beautiful: we might make a similar generalization that old is beautiful. We are said to be heading towards a so-called post-Fordian society where decentralization and creativity are to be the order of the day. That bodes well for the re-use of old buildings by new generations who can work where they please in small groups or alone, linked by cables underground to their confrères elsewhere. Perhaps brave new world will become brave old world; and will be all the better for that.

Chapter 10

THE FUTURE OF THE HERITAGE

We have come a long way from the first heritage legislation of 1882: 8000 conservation areas, 15 000 scheduled ancient monuments and approaching half a million listed buildings are testimony to our growing regard for the built environment. The main effort of recording and classifying the past is now almost complete. The question now is one of what we do with all this information. Now that it has been identified, what is the future of the heritage? In particular, what is the task of the agencies, central and local, private and public, that are involved, and where does the individual owner or developer fit into the picture?

First, we must ask if the task of recording the heritage is complete. In the case of ancient monuments, it seems to be far from ended. English Heritage estimate that the numbers of scheduled ancient monuments should grow to around 30 000 by the end of the Monuments Protection Programme that is now under way. The task here is an urgent one, since so many monuments are vulnerable, either because, like the Rose Theatre in Southwark, they are in the way of proposed new development in city-centre locations where land values are high, or because they are only partially visible in fields and are in constant danger of being ploughed out of existence. The technology of archaeology is now very sophisticated and seems likely to continue to improve. It is quite possible that the recording of ancient monuments will never be quite at an end for the very good reason that advancing technology will give the ancient monuments inspector and the archaeologist new tools with which to detect monuments where none was thought to exist.

Historic buildings are at least visible, although as the resurvey has shown, there is still a certain amount of detective work to do in discovering them in places where they have been overlooked or where their special interest is masked by later additions and alterations. But some of the early greenback resurvey lists are felt by English Heritage to be inadequate and they have made a start on their revision. In these cases, the inadequacy was manifest in the way that the inspectors did not use the criteria properly in the form in which they were revised in 1970. List descriptions were too short and many nineteenth century and even eighteenth century buildings were overlooked. But the wider question is how far the resurvey lists are organic, and should accordingly be updated in the light of recent scholarship, their criteria reworked to reflect public opinion as it changes. The alternative is that they should be regarded as tablets of stone which will stand for a further generation or more. Clearly owners and developers (and planning authorities too for that matter) are entitled to a degree of certainty about whether a building is of special interest or not. Certificates of immunity, as we have seen, contain an element of gamble, and spot-listing is liked by no-one, including the conservationist. And yet, the quality of the lists themselves has changed in the course of the resurvey: the early ones were very thin on Victorian buildings and vernacular buildings and contained no inter-war architecture. It would be unfair and even arrogant to suggest that these lists should not be updated to current standards; and equally unfair and even perverse to suggest that we have now reached the outer limits of architectural scholarship and public taste, and that no further updating will be needed.

The problem of listing modern buildings brings the problem into particular focus. It is probably always desirable in any field where aesthetics and personal tastes are involved to gain a perspective before making judgments on what is or is not of special interest. But we know the pace of change is considerable: the life of even major new buildings can be short if economic conditions and the value of the site dictate that they should be replaced after 10, 20 or 30 years. If we are to preserve the best modern architecture, we must act now. This was the reason for the so-called Skelmersdale rule that any building of recognized outstanding international interest can be listed after only 10 years if there is an imminent threat to it. Even this, which allows for a minimal period of reflection on a building's worth, may not be enough to save some modern buildings.

The more considerable problem in the case of modern buildings is to define exactly what is of special interest. The original tower blocks which had such an influence on the post-war architecture of our cities have a certain historic interest as the precursors of a social and architectural revolution. But the experiment failed. Should we preserve them, as we might preserve the remains of a concentration camp, as a dreadful warning to future generations? Again, should we attempt to list modern buildings that may be seminal in the eyes of architectural historians (or more commonly in the eyes of a section of them) while the public hate them? Does it devalue conservation for it to be associated with items that do not command public affection or respect? The number of modern buildings that have been listed to date have shown that Ministers are taking an understandably cautious approach. Probably no-one would grudge Coventry Cathedral or the Royal Festival Hall their Grade I listings. Most of the others would probably find public favour as examples of the more acceptable face of modern architecture. But there are one or two exceptions: according Grade II* status to the neo-Brutalist *Economist* building in St James was an act of political courage, the more so as it was listed under the Skelmersdale rule. This will understandably remain perhaps the single most controversial aspect of listing policy. Interestingly, it is one which Ministers are seeking to open up to a wider public debate, with a greater degree of public consultation than there is with other listing recommendations.

Scheduling and listing are in the gift of the Secretary of State and are at least capable of central direction. But the designation of conservation areas is a local authority matter and less subject to Departmental control; here, as well, changing tastes will have their effect. Those ideas about the familiar, the well-loved and the totally unlistable we discussed in Chapter 1 come to the fore in this field. Planning authorities can designate any area they like as an areas of special architectural or historic interests, and in this they will be subject to all sorts of local and political pressure. Authorities have not been immune from the accusation that some conservation areas have been designated solely in order to frustrate particular developments where the planning authority felt there was no other way of doing this. Should the Secretary of State take away or at least modify local authorities' powers now that the great mass of designations have taken place? If not, will he be able to allow authorities to update their views of 'special interest' in line with developments on the listing front? We already have the prospect of inter-war housing estates being designated as conservation areas: in time, could we see areas of Stevenage New Town and Milton Keynes going the same way?

The questions are easy to pose; but the answers are harder to give. All we can say is that there is little sign of public opinion's generally pro-conservation line in any way diminishing and that public pressure for increases in the numbers of ancient monuments, listed buildings and conservation areas seems likely to continue. That begs the question of what we are to do with the large numbers of monuments, buildings and areas that we are protecting. Conservation, as we have seen, includes the idea of change so far as this is compatible with special architectural or historic interests. More pressure will be put on developers, architects and planners to find new uses for old buildings and to adapt them to the needs of the last decade of the twentieth century. Government policy on this is clearly set out in PPG15 and seems to be fully in accord with public opinion. In the case of ancient monuments, there will be special problems, for the scope to adapt them to new uses will be limited at best and in many cases non-existent. It is very difficult to make anything of a field monument, and the present arrangements for guardianship and compensation payments may simply have to be extended.

But perhaps the question is most acute in the case of rescue archaeology. Again, there is no prospect of new use and there is in this instance the all too frequent prospect of development pressure of the acutest sort because of the development value of an urban site. The 1979 Act has provided a framework for protection, and PPG16 has established procedures that seem to be working well. But the very fact that archaeological investigation must necessarily proceed while development is taking place will always make this a potentially fraught area.

The machinery for protecting the heritage, once identification has taken place, is rather better. In the last few years, the Department has overhauled the way in which it lists buildings. The code of conduct for fieldworkers and inspectors should ensure that in the majority of cases listing does not come as a nasty shock to owners. The informal appeals mechanism ensures that owners have a right to make representations about the listing of their properties, and the certificate of immunity procedure gives developers the chance to escape the consequences of possible spot-listing altogether. These simple refinements have made the system appear much less heavy handed in its practices and procedures than used to be the case and are much to be welcomed. It is doubtful if spot-listing will ever be altogether avoidable. But the aim should be to make it an exception, rather as the use of building preservation notices are now.

The question in recent years has been in fact whether the pendulum has swung too far in the conservationists' direction. But with the exception of the certificate of immunity procedure, there have been no major modifications to the existing structure of control. Indeed, the Housing & Planning Act 1986 took the opportunity to tighten up the law slightly, while it has been noticeable that the various relaxations of development control introduced in enterprise and simplified planning zones have not been extended to include listed building controls. Similarly, there has been little pressure to reform radically conservation area or ancient monument legislation. The legislative framework seems in fact to be widely regarded as satisfactory, although the Government has shown itself willing to debate its future – for example, over the retention of the full panoply of controls for all Grade II listed buildings.

Where the pressure does exist is on the margin. The position of the churches for instance, as we noted in Chapter 6, is still something of an anomaly. Similarly, an awkward interface continues to exist between listed building controls and fire and building regulations. Clearly, where safety is at stake there is less room for compromise, and publications such as those produced by English Heritage are helpful in seeking a way forward which can satisfy all parties. Then again, although the position in England is clear, resurvey work in Scotland and Wales still has a little way to go, as it has in Northern Ireland. In these parts of the United Kingdom, it is difficult to keep up sometimes with the need to spot-list buildings, and the need for a systematic resurvey must come second.

But the main problem faced by the heritage is the simple one of how to find the means to keep it. The state can and does pay only a fraction of the cost. Private owners are happy to find some of the funds themselves; but they are not always able to do so and they are not always able to find enough money to preserve a building in the way it should be. The problem here is probably less acute than it was a few years ago. For all but a few buildings, it is simply not enough to insist that they be cocooned and preserved at public expense. In order to survive, the heritage must pay its way, and to a very large extent it does. We have charted the growth of moves to find new uses for old buildings, and this continues to be one of the most hopeful signs for the future of conservation. But as the numbers of listed buildings and conservation areas have grown so has the challenge to architects and developers. That challenge will continue and will intensify, particularly in periods of economic growth when development pressures are strong.

The problems can be quite subtle. For instance, many listed buildings lend themselves to conversion for use by small organizations. Such groups tend to stay for short periods due to the riskiness of their businesses and their lack of financial reserves: this in turn gives those financing such projects more problems because the rapid rate of turnover of tenants is less attractive to lenders or investors than the lower turnover of tenants that can be expected with larger organizations occupying modern buildings. The evidence seems to be that much can be achieved where there is a local climate of goodwill. It has been argued, for instance, that effective groundwork produced a better public reaction to pro-conservation policies in Chester in the mid-sixties than was the case in York or Bath.

The size of the problem here was suggested by a pilot study carried out by English Heritage in Kirklees in West Yorkshire. This suggested that there may be as many as 9200 buildings in the top risk category in conservation areas alone – a figure equivalent to over 2% of England's listed buildings. A separate study of Grade I listed buildings in 1994 suggested that 1% were at risk from neglect, and a further 8% were vulnerable and in danger of falling into the same category. English Heritage's appointment of a Buildings at Risk Officer has been an imaginative step in the right direction, and has been accompanied by the beginnings of a national Buildings at Risk register to supplement the many county-wide registers set up by County Councils and voluntary groups. If such buildings can at least be pinpointed and their difficulties be highlighted, that is at least a start, not least because the likelihood of finding someone with the right entrepreneurial flair and technical knowledge locally must be small. Similar work was done by the Department of the Environment's Historic Buildings Bureau, which used to produce registers of difficult-to-sell listed buildings.

These developments are all to the good. They help heritage buildings in every community in the country, including many that are not so distinguished or special that listed or not they might fall into a gentle decline. But there is no doubt that the heritage is also big business. The English Tourist Board now estimates that 79 million people visited heritage buildings in 1990. Westminster Abbey alone attracted 3 million visitors, St Paul's Cathedral 2.5 million and the Tower of London 2.3 million. Just as significantly, 30% of foreign visitors cite our architectural heritage as their sole reason for visiting the United Kingdom, and 70% include it as one of their reasons: in fact, 75% make it to a historic site during their stay. Heritage is a multi-million pound industry and its contribution to the success of tourism in the United Kingdom is undoubted: like it or not, many visitors come to this country because of the images that we mentioned in Chapter 1 – the thatched cottages, the medieval churches and (increasingly) the satanic mills. The purists may not like it. The cynics may sneer at it. But at the end of the day there is a powerful argument for protecting the heritage because it earns its own living.

For impressive as the revenue-earning figures are, one of Britain's main attractions to both her inhabitants and her visitors is that it is a historic country where the heritage is something that can be felt and experienced and even lived in. Not for us the doubtful delights of Williamsburg. We do not have to travel hundreds of miles to Harpers Ferry to experience what a historic town looks like. We may be lucky enough to live in a historic centre. If not, it is almost certain that there will be at least one listed building in the community in which we live. There are more likely to be several, and we may additionally live in or be close to a conservation area. Every ancient monument, every listed building and every conservation area is part of the national heritage and should be honoured as such. They emphasize our continuity with the past and our achievements as a nation and as a series of communities.

The Press Notice which accompanied one junior Environment Minister's speech was headlined 'Heritage is not for Toffs'. Behind this oddly old-fashioned allusion lies the secret of Britain's success in the conservation field. We have a fundamentally democratic approach to heritage questions. The French and the Americans may have an élitist philosophy and concentrate their resources on a relatively small number of *monuments classés* or on their National Landmarks Register. The British, with an architectural heritage still happily largely untouched by war, cherish the ordinary and the mundane, but elevate these to a special status because they have as buildings or areas an interest in the architectural, social or economic history of their country.

And this has had its benefits. If an Englishman's home is his castle, he seems to treasure it even more if it is listed. London estate agents used to reckon that the cachet of listing added an average 10% to the value of a house, and this is certainly reflected in the fact that more applications to spot-list properties come from individual owners than ever stem from local authorities and amenity societies. The whole system of heritage legislation could not have evolved the way it has without commanding public support and reflecting public pressure. Indeed, the designation of conservation areas, which stresses the requirement for public participation, would not have expanded outside the historic centres without a groundswell of public support. Conservation may be parodied as a middle class crusade, but it has received the backing of all classes of society and has an appeal that knows no barriers.

This leaves us with two challenges. The first is to maintain the impetus now that the major work of identifying those parts of the heritage we wish to conserve is substantially complete. The second is to ensure that the heritage continues to be integrated into our way of living and for developers and planners into our way of thinking. As these chapters have shown, we have made substantial progress in both fields. To achieve a synthesis where both challenges can be met is the next task. We do not want a Britain that is a living museum set solely around theme parks and heritage centres: but equally, we are mindful of the damage that has been done to the heritage even within our own lifetimes. To get the balance right in the eyes of everyone will be impossible. To get the balance right in the eyes of the majority should be hard enough. But it is the target towards which perhaps we should aim.

Appendix A

THE CRITERIA FOR LISTING

The criteria for listing were drawn up by the (then) Historic Buildings Council at the outset of the national resurvey of historic buildings. In 1987, the criteria were amended to include post-1939 buildings. PPG15 has further amended the definition.

The criteria have been approved by the Secretary of State. They form a set of general principles of selection, since it would be impossible to prescribe exactly for every case what should and should not be listed.

The criteria for listing are as follows.

All buildings built before 1700 which survive in anything like their original condition.

Most buildings of between 1700 and 1840, though some selection is necessary.

Buildings of between 1840 and 1914 which are the best examples of particular building types, and/or which have definite quality and character. After 1914 selected high quality buildings are listed. These will in general be at least 30 years old, but buildings between ten and 30 years of age may be listed where they are of outstanding quality and they are under threat.

In choosing buildings, particular attention is paid to the following.

Architectural interest All buildings which are of importance to the nation for their architectural design, decoration or craftsmanship or which are important examples of particular building types or techniques and significant plan form.

Historic interest Including buildings illustrating important aspects of the nation's social, economic or cultural history.

Close historical association with nationally important people or events.

Group value Especially where buildings comprise an important architectural or historic unity or a fine example of planning.

Appendix B

LIST OF
ADDRESSES

The following is not claimed to be an exhaustive list of all those bodies with an interest in the built heritage. That could almost be a small book in itself. But it does cover the main bodies, and in particular those which are mentioned in the text.

Architectural Heritage Fund 27 John Adam Street, London WC2N 6HX
    Tel.: 0171-925-0199
Ancient Monuments Society St Ann's Vestry Hall, 2 Church Entry, London EC4V 5AB
    Tel.: 0171-236 3934
Association for Industrial Archaeology Ironbridge, Telford, Shropshire TF8 7AW
    Tel.: 01952 453522
CADW Brunel House, 2 Fitzalan Road, Cardiff CF2 1UY
    Tel.: 01222 465511
Church Commissioners 1 Millbank, London SW1P 3JZ
    Tel.: 0171-222 7010
Civic Trust 17 Carlton House Terrace, London SW1Y 5AW
    Tel.: 0171-930 0914
Council for British Archaeology Bowes Morrell House, 111 Walmgate, York YO1 2VA
    Tel.: 01904 671417
Department of the Environment 2 Marsham Street, London SW1P 3EB
    Tel.: 0171-276 3000
Department of National Heritage 2–4 Cockspur Street, London SW1Y 5DH
    Tel.: 0171-211 6000

Friends of Friendless Churches 12 Edwardes Square, London W8 6HG
Tel.: 0171-602 6267

Georgian Group 37 Spital Square, London E1 6DY
Tel: 0171-377 1722

Historic Buildings and Monuments Commission for England (English Heritage) Fortress House, 23 Savile Row, London W1X 1AB
Tel.: 0171-973 3000

Historic Houses Association 38 Ebury Street, London SW1W 0LU
Tel.: 0171-730 9419

Institute of Advanced Architectural Studies (University of York) The King's Manor, York YO1 2EP
Tel.: 01904 24919

Joint Committee of the National Amenity Societies c/o Ancient Monuments Society, St Ann's Vestry Hall, 2 Church Entry, London EC4V 5AB
Tel.: 0171-236 3934

National Heritage Memorial Fund 10 St James Street, London SW1A 1CF
Tel.: 0171-930 0963

National Trust 36 Queen Anne's Gate, London SW1H 9AS
Tel.: 0171-226 5922

National Trust for Scotland 5 Charlotte Square, Edinburgh EH2 4DU
Tel.: 0131-248 7461

Redundant Churches Fund St Ann's Vestry Hall, 2 Church Entry, London EC4V 5AB
Tel.: 0171-236 3934

Rescue (British Trust for Archaeology) 15A Bull Plain, Hertford, Herts SG14 1DX
Tel.: 01992 58170

Royal Commission on Historical Monuments for England Fortress House, 23 Savile Row, London W1X 2JQ
Tel.: 0171-973 3500

Royal Commission on Historical Monuments for Wales Edleston House, Queens Road, Aberystwyth, Dyfed SY23 2HP
Tel.: 01970 4381

Royal Commission on Historical Monuments for Scotland 52/54 Melville Street, Edinburgh EH3 7HF
Tel.: 0131-225 5994

Royal Institute of British Architects 66 Portland Place, London W1N 4AD
  Tel.: 0171-580 5533

Royal Institution of Chartered Surveyors 12 Great George Street, Parliament Square, London SW1P 3AD
  Tel.: 0171-222 7000

Royal Town Planning Institute 26 Portland Place, London W1N 4BE
  Tel.: 0171-639 9107

SAVE Britain's Heritage 68 Battersea High Street, London SW11 3HX
  Tel.: 0171-228 3336

Scottish Development Department (Historic Buildings Directorate) 20 Brandon Street, Edinburgh EH3 5DX
  Tel.: 0131-226 2570

Society for the Protection of Ancient Buildings 37 Spital Square, London E1 6DY
  Tel.: 0171-377 1644

Twentieth Century Society 58 Crescent Lane, London SW4 9PU
  Tel.: 0171-793 9898

Victorian Society 1 Priory Gardens, London W4 1TT
  Tel.: 0181-994 1019

Appendix C

BIBLIOGRAPHY

Betjeman, J. (1943) *English Cities and Small Towns*, Collins, London.

Binney, M. (1984) *Our Vanishing Heritage*, Arlington Books.

Cunnington, P. (1988) *Change of Use*, Alphabooks.

Department of the Environment (1971) *New Life for Old Buildings*, HMSO, London.

Department of the Environment (1978) *New Life for Old Churches*, HMSO, London.

Dixon, R. and Muthesius, S. (1978) *Victorian Architecture*, Thames & Hudson, London.

Dobby, A. (1978) *Conservation and Planning*, Hutchinson, London.

Esher, Lord (1981) *A Broken Wave*, Allen Lane, London.

Insall, D. (1972) *The Care of Old Buildings Today*, Architectural Press, London.

Kennet, Lord (1972) *Preservation*, Temple Smith.

Ministry of Housing and Local Government (1967) *Historic Towns: Preservation & Change*, HMSO, London.

Parnell, A. (1987) *Building Legislation and Historic Buildings*, Architectural Press, London.

Reynolds, J. (ed.) (1976) *Conservation Planning in Town & Country*, Liverpool University Press, Liverpool.

Richards, J.M. (1940) *An Introduction to Modern Architecture*, Penguin, Harmondsworth, Middx.

Strong, R., Binney, M. and Harris, J. (1974) *The Destruction of the Country House*, Thames & Hudson, London.

Suddards, R. (1988) *Listed Buildings*, Sweet & Maxwell, London.

Watkin, D. (1980) *The Rise of Architectural History*, Architectural Press, London.

Young, G. (1977) *Conservation Scene*, Kestrel.

Articles and circulars

Delafons, J. Planning & Conservation 1909–1932, JPEL June 1994
Department of the Environment Circulars
    86/72 Town & Country Planning (Amendment) Act 1972 – Conservation
    46/73 Conservation & Preservation – Local Government Act 1972
    102/74 Town & Country Planning Act 1971 – Historic Buildings and Conservation
    147/74 Town & Country Amenities Act 1974
    23/77 Historic Buildings and Conservation Areas – Policy and Procedures
    12/81 Historic Buildings and Conservation Areas
    8/87 Historic Buildings and Conservation Areas – Policy and Procedures
Department of the Environment and Department of National Heritage
    Planning Policy Guidance 15 *Planning and the Historic Environment*
    Planning Policy Guidance 16 *Archaeology & Planning*
    Responsibility for Conservation Policy and Casework (DoE Circular 20/92 DNH Circular 1/92)
Department of National Heritage
    What Listing Means – A guide for owners and occupiers
    The Ecclesiastical Exemption – what it is and how it works
English Tourist Board (1988) *English Heritage Monitor 1988*
Jenkins, S. (1981) *The Anger of Firestone*, Thirties Society Journal No. 1.
Ministry of Housing and Local Government Circulars
    53/67 Civic Amenities Act Parts I and II
    61/68 Town & Country Planning Act 1968 – Part V Historic Buildings and Conservation
Picture Post (4 January 1941) *A Plan for Britain.*
Robertson M. *et al. Listed Buildings: the National Resurvey of England*, Transactions of the Ancient Monument Society 1993.
Woof, R. and Gatesby, Ian C. (6 May 1981) *Listed Buildings and the 1980 Planning Act*, Law Society Gazette.

INDEX